LIFE REMODELED

Mark Taylor & Chip Rice

with Jeannie Taylor

Cover Design by Amy George

Published in association with His Story Ministries.
HisStoryMinistries.com

WHAT PEOPLE ARE SAYING ABOUT LIFE REMODELED

Finally, a book and a Bible study for real men (and women)! As Mark and Jeannie take us with them on their raw journey of losing everything in LIFE REMODELED, the reader experiences the emotions of their trauma through the lens of both a male and female perspective. The struggle of building businesses, the pain of seeing their dreams demolished, and finally the process of rebuilding gives all couples hope for the day to day issues they are facing. Mark and Jeannie are resilient, and they learned how to rebuild their lives on the foundation of a relationship with Jesus. LIFE REMODELED is a tool for every marriage toolbox.

— Don Immel, Superintendent, PennDel
Ministry Network (PennDel.org), and wife Robin.

What does success in life look like? Family, business, church all looked good on the surface for Mark Taylor. Read LIFE REMODELED to see how God brought Mark through the crucible of failure to lead him to restore relationship with his wife, family, his career, but most of all with his God. Every man and woman in your church should read this book and talk about this material together.

— David L. Balinski, East Coast Regional Director,
Christian Business Men's Connection (cbmc.com)

LIFE REMODELED is a compelling and honest journey through the potential pitfalls of every leader – male and female. It challenges us to look deep into our own behaviors and motivations, and it offers us a redemptive message for rebuilding our lives on the only firm and sure foundation – Jesus Christ our Lord.

— Doreen Lecheler, Peak Performance Author, Speaker and Consultant (DoreenLecheler.com)

LIFE REMODELED is an amazing account of the faithfulness of God! The theme of God's care for his children is a constant thread through the chapters as Mark and Jeannie recount their journey. It is an encouragement to stop and notice how God has guided each of our lives.

— Dr. Stephen R. Tourville, retired Superintendent, PennDel Ministry Network, and wife Marjorie

With vulnerability and candor, Mark and Jeannie Taylor offer readers a front-row seat to watch God remodel their lives, relationship, and faith...brick by brick. We were moved to tears at the immense pain of their journey and inspired to never give up on life's biggest hopes and dreams. Every couple needs to read LIFE REMODELED together. It will strengthen your marriage as well as your relationship with Christ!

— Shane Wilson, Lead Pastor, Christian Life Assembly (clacamphill.com), and wife Heidi

To Glenn and Phyllis Taylor (Dad and Mom), our daughter Jamie and her husband Gordon, our son Jerry and his wife Anna, and our daughter Joanie and her husband David.

This close-knit family is the greatest blessing in our lives. Your love and support mean more than you know.

ACKNOWLEDGEMENTS

First and foremost, we thank God for inspiring and leading us through the process of writing this book. To Him belongs the glory. We also thank our families for their patience, support, and belief in the importance of this project.

Life Remodeled was greatly improved by insight and contributions from our proofreaders: Jim and Sue-Ellen Edmonds, Shari Rice, Rhonda Marsh, Paul and Robin Eschbach, Pastor Candace Harris, Bill and Kay Wray, David Balinski, and Pastor Tom and Marty (Mary Alice) Willard. Huge thanks to each of you!

Thank you, Amy George, for a wonderful cover and interior layout. Thank you, Pastor Scott Ball, for publishing and design consultation. And thank you, Dave Weikert, for your help with audio/visual and online development.

Finally, we want to thank the entire church family at Christian Life Assembly. So many of you have played significant roles in loving us through hard times, shaping our lives, and supporting our desire to tell His story.

Readers, we thank you, too!
And we would love to hear from you.
HisStoryMinistries.com

CONTENTS

FOREWORD
Chip Rice

When I first began serving on committees with Mark Taylor, I found him witty, insightful, and brimming with enthusiasm. Months later, at Mark's request, we began to meet privately for coffee and conversation, and not until then did I hear portions of the story you now hold in your hands. At once, it gripped me, commanded my attention. Mark sometimes laughed while telling tales about himself. More often, however, he fought off the urge to cry, and I sensed within him a deep remorse and a desire to let his story be used by God, to bare his pain so that others may avoid it. A heart cannot help being touched by such courage, and as a writer I felt moved to enable Mark's goal. He had a story worth telling. One of grit, love, loss, and hope. A story to impact lives, both now and forever.

We were standing in my foyer, fully caffeinated, an hour of conversation still foremost in our minds. As Mark slipped on his shoes, I proposed writing a book. He'd tell the stories; I'd polish and knit them together. Within minutes we'd decided to go for it.

My initial approach was to craft a novel based on the truth. After interviewing Mark, I got some chapters on paper but sensed in my gut a fundamental flaw. Not in the material, but in my means of expressing it. Mark is so genuine, so transparent about his life, that portraying it dramatically and with literary freedom felt like a betrayal of purpose. Mark loves to talk, laugh, and shoot straight about the lessons he's learned. And I gradually realized that any book about him must be equally authentic, sometimes funny, and totally straightforward. I was writing reality, not a made-for-TV movie.

When I shared my concern, Mark already felt likewise. He'd recently talked with a pastor who writes in a tone of casual conversation, and he desired the same for our book. So we agreed at once to discontinue the novel and deliver Mark's story in a more relaxed and honest way. God had united our perspectives without either of us knowing, and we really began to sense His anointing on the project.

I'm not sure if we accomplished casual conversation—a definite stretch for my writing style—but I can promise you this: What you're about to read is absolutely true. Nothing added, no embellishments. It's a first-hand account of a life remodeled, and I pray it moves your heart as it has mine. For whether reading or writing it, Mark Taylor's journey to Jesus is compelling.

Your eternity, like his, may never be the same.

INTRODUCTION

Remodeling begins with demolition. Out with the old, in with the new. Buildings are razed, spaces gutted, only to be recrafted with improved form and function. It's the essence of my trade. It is also, I believe, essential to life. Our most meaningful lessons, those that alter who we become and the paths we take, often begin with some form of demolition. The challenge thereafter is to rise above the wrecking ball, to refuse to wallow in the dust and rubble of shattered pursuits, flawed perspectives; careless decisions, or broken relationships.

Trust me; I'm living proof.

My wrecking ball struck in 2003, making dust and rubble of countless poor choices I'd stacked one upon another. Following impact I lived without friends, kept my family at a distance. Day by day, in a darkened room, I did little more than sit on a couch, devoid of hope, riddled by guilt, and pierced by one tiny yet enormous question: How?

How did I get to this point...descend to this depth...lose so much? How?

The Foundation
CHAPTER ONE

About ninety miles north of Pittsburgh, Oil City is now a gray comparison to the vibrant town in which I'd been raised. In the 1960's and 70's it was corporate headquarters to oil-industry giants Pennzoil and Quaker State. Jobs flourished, the community buzzed, but the health of our city was tenuous, tethered mostly to oil production. When the big corporations pulled up stakes, they uprooted many lives and nearly toppled our region. Oil City managed to hold on, pulling tight to its bootstraps, but never recovered the charm or color I'd experienced as a kid.

Back in our proverbial good old days, my mom stayed home with my brother and me, secure in the income of my father, a banker, who also happened to be a do-it-yourself man. Dad took care of everything around the house, even when he wasn't sure where to begin. Helping him to build and figure things out, I developed a love for design and remodeling. And before long, no matter the task, Dad could always count on my hands in the mix. Or perhaps fear them. I remember many times when he completed work first and then whistled for my brother and me to help clean up. Those scenarios really irritated me, but after raising my own children I totally understand a father's need to work alone sometimes.

One place we were never alone was at church. Sunday mornings I'd impatiently wait as my parents talked after service. I had friends there too, and we enjoyed hanging out. Like my father, I sang in Sunday choir and performed as a vocalist at weddings and events. Sometimes we'd even sing a duet, my most cherished musical memories. My family rarely made it home for an NFL kickoff, but looking back I understand how spending time with people at church contributed much to my upbringing.

Dad's examples in church and lessons at home were just two of the ways his life shaped mine. We also had our share of spats, and as a disciplinarian true to his generation, he whipped my butt more times than I remember. But beyond our requisite father-son sparring, what I saw in my dad—at home, at church, in the community—was a leader, a man who inspired and motivated me. I don't mean to imply that we sat together and discussed such things over coffee, for that was never his style. Dad's life lessons simply took root in me as I observed and lived under his leadership.

He became Senior Vice President of the bank where he worked. He was Chairman of the Board for the Oil City Hospital, our church board president, and a member of several other organizations. In each of these roles he conducted himself in a down-to-earth manner that resonated with people. This does not mean, however, he withheld feelings or opinions. Quite the opposite. A determined straight shooter, Dad spoke up when something wasn't right, but his correction was always delivered with care, and that's what set him apart. In social situations he was equally graceful. I especially admired his ability to balance serious conversation with playful harassment. In almost any setting or circumstance, Dad was a man who truly loved people, who cared about their lives and well-being. I may not have articulated it so well as a boy, but I understood even then how much he valued relationships.

Foremost among them, his marriage.

Dad loved my mother deeply. She was his queen and our expectations were clear: treat Mom with respect or face the wrath of Dad. He bought her things from time to time, but what impressed me most were the thoughtful words and gestures by which he communicated love. Dad tried so hard to honor his wife and bring the best out of her by consistently living as the man she needed him to be. He met her every need, and I never saw my mother cry. Well, almost never...

I was in my teens. Our family was preparing for a move in Oil City. Mom had just purchased a padded toilet seat—a trend of the day—but my dad had refused her request to move it. That morning, preparing for school, I discovered my mother alone in the dining room, tissue in hand, crying. I cautiously approached, braced for tragic news.

"Mom... What's wrong?"

"Your father won't let me move the padded toilet seat."

Well, as you might imagine, life moved on, and this tale has become a Taylor family classic. I suppose we men do all have our quirks, but aside from this unfortunate toilet seat standoff, my dad was a great husband, and from him I learned as much about marriage as I did about leadership.

Over the years, many have expressed admiration for my father and what he meant to the Oil City community, and I suppose what I respect most about my dad, the part of him I love to emulate, is less about his methods and more about the outcome of his heartfelt way with people. What I mean is: From family to friends to subordinates, Dad made everyone around him better. This to me is his greatest personal asset, and it will no doubt rest at the heart of his soon-to-be legacy. At age 86, Glenn R. Taylor is in the final stages of Alzheimer's disease. He has forgotten all about what I've just written.

Those whose lives he touched have not.

The Fracture
CHAPTER TWO

Despite the admiration I held for my father, he and I differed in one significant way: employment. Dad was always content to spend his days in an office, working under the authority of a boss. I, on the other hand, knew early in life that a similar path was not for me. I would live independently, work with my hands, design and create in a variety of environments, and support myself along a self-chartered course. My heart beat with optimism, ambition, and ideas.

Wisdom, on the other hand, eluded me.

Now, to say I lacked wisdom, of course, is hindsight. When I graduated high school in 1976 I had wisdom enough to traverse the continent, fly to the moon, or even broker world peace. I settled for a two-year architectural degree at Penn State's Shenango Valley Campus.

Honestly, I didn't really want to go to college. As a student, I felt restless, unfit for formal education. I struggled to learn via books or lectures, much preferring the hands-on experience of designing or building or just figuring things out on my own. Such activities seemed to develop my brain in sustainable ways. But for a Taylor, college was expected, closed to discussion, a monkey I needed off my back. So I muddled my way through the papers and textbooks. And architecture, I discovered, was indeed a good fit for my career ambitions. I especially enjoyed the drafting process and my part-time work with a campus-area construction company, from which I learned as much on the job as I did in the classroom. During summer breaks, I helped to frame houses with an Oil City contractor, also an excellent learning experience. Finally, in 1978, I left Shenango Valley with degree in hand.

Holding the other was the love of my life.

I met Jeannie three months prior to graduation, at a college party. She wasn't a student but a local resident who worked at an ice cream cone factory—not filling cones but actually making them. It took only one look and a few clumsy words for me to enter into orbit over her. In fact, that night I tried so hard to impress Jeannie that I invited her parachuting, knowing quite well I would never have the guts to jump from an airplane. True story. Thank goodness, she never called me to task.

The following day I asked two of Jeannie's friends to invite her to a party planned for later that week. Another so soon? Well, this was college, and my roommates and I could always find something to celebrate. If I recall correctly, this may have been the "Third Thursday after Ground Hog Day" party, but I digress. More on point: Jeannie accepted my invitation, and that night I eagerly met her at the door where, after seeing my face, she finally remembered who I was. No kidding. What a great first impression I must've made! Scratch parachute boasting from the pick-up line playbook. Nevertheless, the night went well, and my interest in Jeannie soared to higher levels. I sensed her feelings were mutual when she suggested we travel together to visit her sister in Texas.

Before meeting Jeannie I'd gone home every weekend, but I spent my last semester on campus with her. She even did my laundry, an aggressive step toward exclusivity. We fell in love easily, found our families similar, and I knew without question Jeannie was the one.

After graduation I returned to Oil City and worked in construction.

Jeannie stayed in Shenango Valley, continuing her factory job. Man, was that a tough arrangement! We talked every night, dated every weekend, but it wasn't enough. Adding fuel to the fire was our escalating itch for adventure. Our jobs were boring, and we longed to experience life beyond our hometowns. So, again, Jeannie suggested we travel to Texas, this time proposing we actually move in with her sister, who seemed open to the idea. Jeannie's father had a connection in Austin at the Westinghouse Corporation, granting Jeannie access to potential job openings. Convinced the odds were in our favor, we wasted no time packing.

Long story short, Westinghouse needed drafting personnel but had no openings for Jeannie. So, they hired me while she took a job at K-Mart. Not what we'd expected, but we hardly cared a bit. Texas was a blast, and our life together had officially begun. We married four months later, with twelve people in attendance, and that same year our first daughter Jamie was born.

A Word from Jeannie...

I was seeing two other guys when I met Mark.

Sounds crazy, but neither relationship was serious. One of the guys I knew from high school. We'd gone to dinner and a movie, but I was just being nice, not really feeling it. The second was a guy in whom I had much more interest, the super-cute younger brother of my best friend's brother-in-law. Go ahead, read that again.

Many of my friends attended Penn State's Shenango Valley Campus, which was also the place to party for local teens. And that's where I first met Mark, at a college party. The night got crazy, as parties tend to do, and I honestly didn't remember him or his supposed invitation to go parachute jumping. Although knowing him now, I can totally believe it!

When two friends invited me to attend another party at Mark's request, I literally said, "Who?" Zero recollection! But I sure was curious. So, I accepted his blind invitation and did recognize Mark when he greeted me. I liked him immediately, very much drawn to his humor and charm. He was kinda cute, too, and from that night forward I dated only him.

I knew my attraction to Mark was strong when I invited him to Texas on only our second date. He said yes, but in planning for the trip I learned my sister in Austin was actually open to the idea of live-in company. So, rather than visit I decided to move there, eager to leave small-town PA and the drudgery of working at the George & Thomas Cone Company. Of course, I just had to bring Mark. It was the liberal 70's, after all, and I was head-over-heels in love with the guy. To my delight, he accepted, and my sister, bless her heart, agreed to two house guests.

Just nineteen and twenty, our lifetime journey had begun.

In Texas, Mark took a job drafting while I worked at K-Mart. Within months we were married, expecting a child, and in need of our own apartment. We chose one on the second floor of a complex near my sister's house. Only one bedroom, but with plenty of light and very cool cathedral ceilings. And, dare I mention, cockroaches, palm-sized spiders, and scorpions fond of hiding in my laundry! But Austin culture was a blast, and we loved each other enough to pull through those crazy newlywed days.

Until Jamie was born, and homesickness got the better of us both.

I was twenty-one. Jeannie was twenty. Our parents lived sixteen-hundred miles away. And into our apartment we'd just brought a newborn.

Awestruck, we stared at precious little Jamie as she wriggled on our bed. Thirty minutes later, she began to cry. Clueless and panic-stricken, I looked up at Jeannie, and what happened next I will never forget. In a stunning display of motherly instinct, my wife lifted and comforted our baby. Like me, she'd had no practice, no previous experience. But in that critical moment she calmed Jamie and me. Her inclinations as a mother have amazed me ever since.

New home, new state, new jobs, new marriage, new daughter. Life was happening fast—too fast! And parenting seemed to awaken in us a fresh sense of how much we valued extended family. For some much-needed help, certainly, but also for sentimental reasons. You see, Jamie was the first grandchild on both sides, and we wanted our parents to easily and routinely be involved in her life, especially around the holidays. The internet had not been invented, which meant no Facebook or any of today's online options for staying connected. Worse, we had no phone. Our calls to home were made collect from Jeannie's sister's, and only on Sundays. Growing evermore homesick, I agreed to leave Texas and move in with my in-laws. Yes, returning to Pennsylvania really mattered that much! Joking aside, living with Jeannie's parents was a pleasant and practical short-term arrangement. They made coming home possible, and we sure felt grateful.

Back in PA, I spent a few months in construction before landing a job in the small town of Franklin, on the banks of the Allegheny River. Joy Manufacturing, a producer of heavy mining equipment, had hired me as a drafter. Not computer-aided drafting mind you; we're talking paper, pencil, scale, and compass. But I loved every minute of expressing mechanical concepts in detail, and I couldn't get enough of illustrating pieces and the intricate ways they worked together. The job fit me like a glove. Better still, it allowed Jeannie and me to afford an apartment. We chose one a few miles northeast of Franklin, in a familiar place called Oil City.

Who says you can never go home again?

Although I loved the drafting aspects of working for Joy Manufacturing, I grew weary of sitting in a cubicle. Many were the days when I dreamed about the wild frontier of self-employment, but leaving my job felt poorly timed and irresponsible. My family was young, and like it or not, cubicle days were a necessary weight upon my shoulders. When our son Jerry was born in 1981, my employment at Joy became even more important to the health of our growing family. So, to compensate for office drudgery, I started moonlighting on remodeling projects wherever and whenever possible. Evenings and weekends, I'd accept almost any job, partly for the money but mostly because I loved the work. Like my dad, I came alive to remodeling challenges, unprepared but with a boatload of confidence.

In time, Jeannie and I moved to a rental house on the banks of the Allegheny River. In springtime and summer the location was beautiful. Jeannie walked the kids daily amid the charm of boats and the excitement of watersports. Winters, however, became desolate, almost imprisoning. I drove our only car to work, which sometimes caused Jeannie and the kids to go weeks without leaving the house. So, we decided to move into town.

My additional income from remodeling projects, as well as FHA loans for first-time home buyers, enabled us to afford a two-bedroom Cape Cod in Oil City, away from the river. We first offered $5,000 below asking price. No deal. Two days later our agent called to say the sellers really liked us, despite the joke I'd made about watering their orange flowered wall paper. Hey, I found it funny…still do!

For a negotiated price, the house became ours. Greeting us there were two lovely neighbors, a retired couple with whom we became close friends. Our table was often set with the delicious food and baked goods they joyfully provided. They supported Jeannie and loved our children, and the man was an avid hunter. Our mutual interest in the great outdoors would often pave the way to more meaningful conversations, usually spiritual. Their Christian faith was strong, and they expressed it in ways that sometimes felt weird, sometimes comforting, but always intriguing. Although we've lost touch, their impact on our lives endures even today.

After one year of living in our Oil City house, Jeannie became pregnant with our third child, and I got laid off from Joy Manufacturing. Twice. Fortunately, my remodeling reputation brought in enough side jobs to keep us afloat. But these projects also increased my courage to attempt self-employment. After each layoff I'd return for the paychecks but discover in my heart a growing distaste for the corporate environment: sitting in a cubicle, answering to a boss, enduring company politics. I understood how a cubicle led to an office as a young drafter worked his way to management. I respected the model, saw how it served my father well in the banking world. But to me it felt suffocating, like a burden I could no longer bear. So, in May of 1984, simply and resolutely, I started Taylor Construction.

Now, by "started" I mean little more than establishing a name, printing some business cards, and thereby attempting to land side jobs in a slightly more official capacity. But this small step proved big enough to crystalize my entrepreneurial drive. Business ownership was my future, my destiny. My hands had gripped the reigns of freedom and self-sufficiency, and I wasn't about to let go. Acting as Taylor Construction, I bid on four projects, vowing to Jeannie that if at least three came through I would resign from Joy Manufacturing.

I got three of the four.

A Word from Jeannie...

Mark loved to build things.

He often shared with me his distaste for working in an office and answering to a boss. And he was never happy behind a desk, always wanting to be out pounding nails. For Mark, the idea of owning a remodeling business was so exciting!

Honestly I only shrugged my shoulders when he told me, feeling somewhat indifferent. I was a mom with two children and one on the way. Mark brought home the bacon, and how he did it was up to him.

I trusted my husband.

Taylor Construction!

My heart flooded with pride and enthusiasm. I even went out and hired a guy. Family tradition was not about to hinder me, and the world couldn't stop me if it tried. The corporate grind could choke on my remodeling dust. Mark Taylor had become a business owner, and it was nothing short of exhilarating.

It was also a large, uncalculated risk.

With minimal forethought and no consultation, I'd sacrificed income, benefits, vacation, and holidays. I'd abandoned the model of my father and many other professionals—one of regular paychecks, covered medical, and manageable time off. And I'd done so with a wife, two children, and one on the way.

But as Ben Franklin wisely said, "Nothing ventured, nothing gained." To embrace risk in pursuit of one's dream is a noble undertaking. What I didn't understand is that determination alone will fail the dreamer. What's required is thoughtful persistence. No matter how passionately a man desires to achieve his goals, patience, humility, and a willingness to learn must underscore his drive, providing a new and firm foundation upon which to anchor his pursuit.

In May of 1984, when I began Taylor Construction, I possessed neither patience nor humility. In my mind, I was an entrepreneur. Realistically, I was a carpenter. A darn good one! But only a carpenter who'd leapt into business, unprepared to lay a new foundation, yet willing to fracture the one upon which my family stood.

The Climb

CHAPTER THREE

Taylor Construction lasted only six months.

I landed plenty of projects throughout the summer, but my nerves became rattled by the onset of colder weather, when remodeling projects tend to decline. Our third child, Joanie, brought additional urgency to my need for financial stability, but I had no savings, no rainy-day fund, and despite success to this point, future work was uncertain. I began to lack confidence (a strange twist, I know!) that Taylor Construction could sustain my family through the harsh winters of western PA.

Conveniently, Zimmerman Homes, a large regional builder, needed a framing contractor. I knew how to frame houses, and Zimmerman was building enough in the area to provide consistent, dependable, year-round employment. I applied for the position, interviewed well, and got offered the unexpected opportunity to open and manage a new office in Clarion, commutable from our home in Oil City. A management position with no need to relocate! I readily accepted…for eight thousand less than I'd been making at Joy Manufacturing. A little salt in my entrepreneurial wound, I suppose.

Now, here's a crazy story: My first day on the job, my first day, I was riding around with a Zimmerman supervisor, just trying to learn the ropes, when we heard about a trophy deer in a nearby hollow, visible from the road. My supervisor looked at me and sheepishly said, "I think

I might shoot that deer." My dumbfounded expression must've seemed approving, or at least nonthreatening, because next thing I knew this guy drove to his house, retrieved his rifle, and sped to the reported location. Sure enough, there stood a beautiful buck. Uncomfortable to say the least, I didn't know whether to interfere or stay silent around this obvious nut case. I can only hope, as of this writing, that the statute of limitations on being party to a poaching has long since expired!

As I grew into this new position, I found myself doing everything short of hands-on construction—office management, marketing, sales, material ordering, even serving as an onsite supervisor. It was trial by fire, thrown in with both feet. Another Zimmerman office in the town of Dubois became a valuable resource and place to get advice, but even so the amount of work was insane. We built houses within such a large radius that traveling from one site to another could take an hour or longer. I felt like I was constantly driving. And remember: This is before cell phones or pagers or even FAX machines. If I missed talking in person I'd spend evenings on the phone. I worked twelve to fourteen hours every day, which was certainly not family friendly.

At home, life became survival. I was the breadwinner, Jeannie the homemaker, with three young children (as cute as they were) filling our world with clutter and noise. Jeannie, of course, endured most of the child rearing. I loved my family and wanted to be home, but working for Zimmerman consumed me, always running here and there, talking hours on the phone. If I wasn't on the job physically, I was there in my mind, spending every waking hour thinking and worrying. My position had no time clock, no punching out for the day. I managed the schedules of all other employees and carried the burden of satisfying customers. The success of our office and the projects we undertook rested squarely on my shoulders. Stress escalated far above what I'd experienced at Joy Manufacturing, while my pay checks, mind you, were thirty percent less. For extra cash, I refereed wrestling with time I didn't have. I became short tempered, a bristly man at work and home. A grouch of a dad. A distant husband. And making matters worse, Jeannie and I had grown tired of Oil City.

As I said in chapter one, Oil City is far from the town it used to be, and by 1984, when I began working for Zimmerman Homes, our fabled community had already lost much of its vibrancy. Jeannie and I had plenty of friends, many through church, where I continued to attend and sing as time permitted. Nevertheless, we believed moving was in our best interest. In our minds, life in Oil City was stagnant, given over to a pattern of monotonous living which no longer appealed to us, especially as parents. We wanted our children to spread their wings and pursue their dreams. We desired a prosperous, energized community. A place of progress and optimism. And we were about to get our wish.

On a hot July evening in the summer of '86, I eagerly told Jeannie about Zimmerman's desire for someone to open an office in the capital city of Harrisburg, a place I'd never even visited. She was equally enthused, and with Jeannie on board I told my boss the next day that I wanted the position. He then told me to write a letter of interest, which I did, and the Zimmerman owner soon called me to his office. Our conversation lasted all of three sentences.

"Mark, I hear you're interested in going to Harrisburg."

"Yes, sir, I am."

"Okay. Done."

It was literally that short.

The company helped move us to the "big city" of Camp Hill, just across the Susquehanna River from Harrisburg. They also paid half our rent for the 3000-square-foot rancher I'd chosen. We could barely furnish it, but standing curbside, nobody knew. I felt so proud to be living in such a spacious and attractive home, but like some of my career moves, I'd selected this house impulsively, without considering...well... much of anything other than making a social statement. Boy was I in for a shock come winter, when our electric furnace produced a $350 bill. In 1986! Thereafter, we spent many frigid nights under blankets near the fire place. Live and learn.

My daytimes, by contrast, generated plenty of heat. Chugging coffee and choking down worries, I'd buzz around the area like a man possessed, logging plenty of miles in my company-owned Ford Ranger. The new Harrisburg branch was to start from square one. Zimmerman owned the land. Beyond that, all other duties were assigned to me. I found the necessary contractors and material suppliers, arranged the building of a spec house, connected with realtors to start the selling process...and those were only the big tasks! All before the advent of modern technology. The hours and leg work were hectic, grueling, borderline unhealthy. But managing the Harrisburg office paid well and would likely lead to corporate advancement. For me, that made it all worthwhile.

As I attacked my schedule, Jeannie built friendships and made social connections in our new community. We selected a church to attend on Sunday mornings. I also sang there occasionally, but due to work demands my involvement was minimal. Jeannie, however, with two children in school and Joanie well beyond the baby stage, found plenty of time to participate in church and other activities that brought her joy and health. And as time marched on, despite those monstrous heating bills, life for my family was generally good. We loved the area, the schools, and the people we'd met. My career, although demanding, seemed stable enough for us to feel grounded, at peace, optimistic about our future in the Harrisburg area. So, I took on the task of building yet another home.

This time for my family.

The decision to build felt appropriate and downright exciting. Finding affordable land was a challenge, but a few lots eventually surfaced. The first one we looked at, though nice, sat adjacent to an interstate highway, a location Jeannie outright refused. The second was a three-acre lot on an undeveloped cul-de-sac in Mechanicsburg. The crisp autumn day on which we saw the property accentuated its beauty, and when I counted seven pheasants in the freshly cut stalks of a nearby cornfield, I was sold. Jeannie agreed, and three months later we broke ground on our dream house. Zimmerman loaned us a down payment, and I worked like a maniac to make it all happen, spending every day managing company projects, then working nights on my own.

The house itself was based on plans from the first Zimmerman home I'd ever seen. Out of all the homes I'd taken part in constructing, this one remained my favorite. After seeing the plans, Jeannie fell for them as well. The design featured cathedral ceilings as well as other amenities. My favorite feature was the screened-in porch overlooking our backyard and the fields through which I walked our dogs. Jeannie absolutely loved the kitchen, especially the peninsula counter top. She called the color terracotta but to me it was orange. Jeannie did everything on that peninsula, from wrapping presents to folding laundry to, of course, serving most of our meals.

If you'll permit me a boast, we simply built a great house. And in it we raised three wonderful children who filled our hearts with the kinds of moments and memories that never leave a family, no matter where life takes them.

A Word from Jeannie...

Building a home was my dream come true.

We were about to break ground on three acres...so much land! I could picture the house before construction even started. We'd chosen the plan for its cathedral ceilings, reminiscent of our first apartment. Ever since our brief stint in Texas, Mark and I had agreed that if we ever built a house it would have cathedral ceilings.

I was so excited to build a home from the ground up, just as our parents had done. But the process called for so many decisions— exterior colors, interior colors, flooring, cabinetry, lighting, hardware, trim... Well, that was an easy one: Stained oak. In our young minds we were sparing no expense.

At the peak of our cathedral ceilings we installed an octagon window with a beautiful stained-glass inset. And my kitchen was an absolute dream. I had an eight-foot peninsula which could seat the whole family, and an oversize pantry with bi-fold doors, behind which were two bottom shelves, a working counter top, and three other shelves to store daily dishes. In fact, the toaster oven, mixer, cookbooks, and coffee pot were stored in there also! The best part: If my pantry was messy when someone came to visit, all I had to do was close the doors, and the kitchen looked instantly presentable.

I also remember how excited Mark and I were to purchase furniture, most of which came from Unclaimed Freight, where we actually found a large, solid oak entertainment center for only $700, because of a scratch on the back! This piece was beautiful and perfectly displayed our twenty-seven-inch Sony TV which, *though obsolete today, was then a joy to behold whether on or off. Over the years, I displayed many framed memories in our entertainment center, and each Christmas I'd cover its top with a snow-covered village of trees, lighted houses, and a variety of figures. The scene grew every year.*

To the family room we added a couch, a loveseat, and a rocker-recliner, something Mark had always wanted. Little did he know, however, that Jerry spent quite a few days in Daddy's chair, wooden spoons tucked in the cushions, pretending to be a pilot while watching VHS recordings of Top Gun or other aviation movies. Joanie preferred our big furry bean bag. Almost every day she would come home from kindergarten, eat lunch, and plop down for Sesame Street or Mr. Roger's Neighborhood, often falling asleep in the bean bag.

The screened-in back porch felt like everyone's favorite part of the house. When building, we'd poured a large concrete slab and embedded within it a birth-year penny for each of our children. It took a few years to finally get the porch covered, but the plan we selected was awesome, with a two-foot-high wall surrounding the slab, a full screen above the wall, and a door leading out to the yard. Funny story: One of the ceiling panels had been walked on, leaving footstep impressions, but we hung it anyway, joking at parties that we loved the porch so much it had us dancing on the ceiling. Oh, the laughs we got over that one! Usually followed by a poor rendition of Lionel Ritchie.

Fortunately, a client of Mark's was building a new deck and offered us some lightly-used patio furniture. Expensive stuff, in great condition. We added outdoor carpeting, folding tables, rope lighting, a dart board, and of course a nice grill. A custom wooden sign was created to read "Taylor Family, established 1978."

I'd often sit on the porch with unsweetened tea, reading a book or clipping coupons, our beagle Brandy resting in a nearby chair (which she considered hers). Better, when the kids were in bed I'd slip out, light candles, and spend time alone reading, praying, or just soaking in the quiet. The back porch was definitely a social hub, but for me it was also a sanctuary, especially when life turned difficult.

Along with tranquility, our three-acre lot brought plenty of yardwork. In the early years, mowing was my responsibility and something I enjoyed, for exercise and a chance to tan. We seemed to have more rocks than grass, so mowing was a tedious and sometimes dangerous job. But I enjoyed the challenge of grooming the lawn, especially as the grass thickened with age and care. It was peaceful, relaxing, good for a mother's soul. Until Mark got a big honkin' riding mower. After that, we'd fight about who got to use it. Men and their toys! That thing was so loud I could hear him mowing from a neighborhood away, walking our dog to cool my temper at having lost the chance to drive it myself.

Such stupid arguments.

Tempers also flared around Memorial Day, which became known to our children as mulching weekend. We had many beds for flowers and shrubs, and therefore bought a ton of mulch. The kids dreaded every minute of prepping and spreading it, but they always stepped up, edging, weeding, raking, and constantly disagreeing about who would drive the tractor pulling trailer loads of mulch. Even today they talk about the "joy" of mulching weekends.

We also had loads of fun on our property, which included a tetherball pole and a basketball hoop and plenty of acreage for sports activities, which we all enjoyed. The competition was serious, too, because I was the type of mother who didn't believe in letting kids win. My dad had been the same, whether shooting hoops or racing me across the yard on his speedy chicken legs. The challenge to beat him always made me try harder, and I wanted the same for my children. Oh, I'd let them catch up, keep the score close, but until they beat me legit, this mamma wasn't going down!

We also had a trampoline on which I loved to teach the kiddos my bouncing tricks, including how to back flip. We'd laugh and jump away hours on end, enjoying each other and the chance to stay active. Of course, when parents weren't home, the trampoline was off limits. But as they say, when the cat's away... Our neighbors called from the hospital to inform us that Jerry had broken his ankle, jumping without supervision.

As time passed and our kids lost interest, the trampoline served as a therapy tool for a young neighbor with autism. He would bounce for a while, crawl under the trampoline to talk with his therapist, then emerge again for more bouncing. This pattern would sometimes continue for hours, and I loved to watch from a distance.

Some of the best fun we had was playing kickball in the cul-de-sac. In warmer seasons, neighborhood kids would gather after supper to set up bases, choose sides, and begin the game. Many parents also came out to join in the game or simply spend time in the cheerful atmosphere. Throughout the year we hosted picnics and parties, some for friends and neighbors, others for Mark's employees. We even hosted our oldest daughter's wedding rehearsal dinner, a precious gathering we still talk about today. No matter the occasion, our get-togethers were always full of laughter. I remember one cookout when Mark placed prime rib on the grill and then walked the guys to a new pen he'd built for

> *his hunting dogs, talking up his work in typical fashion. When*
> *he finally turned around, the grill was completely in flames, and*
> *I've never seen my man run faster. He certainly seared the prime*
> *rib! Fortunately, after slow cooking the flame-encrusted meat, it*
> *turned out delicious.*
>
> *As the years clicked by, I only fell deeper in love with our house*
> *and the memories made there. Memories I planned to surround*
> *myself with as the children grew up and moved on. Memories*
> *I hoped to relive with grandkids, savoring the blessing of deep-*
> *running roots.*
>
> *Mark and I had built our forever home.*

About a year after completing our house, I saw an advertisement for a new community near Lancaster, PA. The builder was Toll Brothers, and they needed a project manager. Now, I know what you're thinking: A job change so soon after building a house? And that's fair criticism. But real or perceived, at that point in time, I simply had a need to branch out. My full-throttled ambition had me seeing greener grasses and believing I'd outgrown my position with Zimmerman. What's more, Lancaster was commutable from our newly-built home. Why not leap? Why miss an opportunity to grow my career?

I applied for the position without even attempting to learn more about Toll Brothers. We were living pre-internet, I was busy as ever, and I didn't have time to dig for details. To be blunt, I really didn't care. A reputable builder sought a new project manager. For ambitious me, that was enough...or so I thought. After applying I privately shared the news with an insulation contractor who in turn exclaimed, "Toll Brothers! Do you know what Toll Brothers is?"

"Not really."

"National Builder of the Year!"

Okay, perhaps a little research had been in order.

Regardless, the National Builder of the Year soon called me for an interview at which we talked mostly about marketing and why I love the construction industry. Asked if I had any further questions, I boldly said, "I guess I'd like to know how I did." The interviewer paused before remarking that he'd never been asked such a question. Then, after another moment of reflection, he affirmed my interview and scheduled a second. Within weeks, I'd landed the job.

My income nearly doubled, and I savored the upward mobility of working for Toll Brothers. In addition to bigger money, I received a car allowance, a formal office, and an administrative assistant. Even started wearing ties! My vice president, a graduate of Wharton Business School at the University of Pennsylvania, was only one step down from company owner Bob Toll, with whom I had much interaction. Each Toll Brothers community was set up like an independent corporation. I was responsible for everything pertaining to the community I managed. Profit and loss were my responsibility, and corporate execs required frequent reports.

Now, here's a humorous snippet: My third day on the job I was called to join these execs at a quarterly project review meeting. Naturally I decided to dress very well, make a good first impression in my slacks, tie, and sport jacket. But entering the boardroom I saw only men in three-piece suits, seated around an enormous table. I was completely underdressed! Worse, they directed me to sit beside Bob Toll himself, who immediately shook my hand, and said, "So, Mark, stand up and tell us about your community." My heart in my throat, I fumbled my way through a satisfactory presentation. And wore a suit to every meeting thereafter.

Of the twenty-seven project managers employed by Toll Brothers,

I was the only one without a bachelor's degree, but the experience I gained there more than made up for it. A few years at Toll Brothers felt equivalent to earning a master's degree in the home-building industry. Perhaps that's why, when the housing market declined in our area, I had the confidence to suggest Toll Brothers sell their Lancaster properties to local builders and shift focus to more successful areas. And perhaps my assertive suggestion inspired them to ask me, Mark Taylor, to launch a new community in Exton, on the outskirts of Philadelphia.

Blinded by another opportunity, I wasted no time arranging a weekend in Exton. Jeannie and I toured the area, met with a realtor, and walked through some houses. Unfortunately, those in our price range were small, disappointing, nowhere near as nice as our Mechanicsburg split-level. We also choked on the high cost of living, sulked about pulling our kids out of school, and questioned the wisdom of moving farther from our families and the community we loved. By noon on Saturday we'd clearly decided a move to Exton was wrong for us. Harrisburg was home, and Exton was too far from it.

Nevertheless, Toll Brothers planned to abandon my communities.

Per my own suggestion!

Whatever could I do?

My Business, Period

CHAPTER FOUR

G reg and I attended church together, where admittedly our
conversations often turned to work. A prominent business owner,
Greg was approachable, wise, and authentic. He was without question
the first and only person I wanted to talk to about my situation.

Fortunately, soon after our trip to Exton, Greg invited my family to
a gathering at his house. That evening I pulled him aside and explained
everything, put it all out there: my present concerns, my passion for
the home-building industry, my career path to date. He graciously
listened, asked some clarifying questions, then advised that I start my
own business.

And a chorus of angels sang 'round about us!

"I don't have the money," I said, snuffing my enthusiasm.

"But, I do," he countered. "What could you do?"

"Well, I've always dreamed of owning my own remodeling business."

"Excellent. Draw up a plan. Let's review it together."

We shook hands, and my feet barely touched the ground until
morning. The idea of launching a business frolicked in me like a
newborn puppy, commanding my attention, driving me mad, and
yet capturing my heart to such an extent that I would do anything to
nurture it. My experience at Toll Brothers had taught me a lot about
managing a business, much more than I'd previously understood. Plus,

starting a business would provide a respectable reason to turn down Exton.

I called my business Taylor Home Remodeling, and my overall plan appealed to Greg, who offered as expected to invest in the company. When I informed Toll Brothers that I would not relocate, my boss asked me to reconsider, assuring me the company would cover expenses and make sure my move was a lucrative one. I declined. He then took me to Bob Toll, who also asked for reconsideration. But my mind was made up. The groundwork was in place. Despite their tempting offers, I walked away from Toll Brothers to pursue a second chance at entrepreneurship.

This time I was ready. The sky was my limit.

Now, it's worth mentioning here that Jeannie neither questioned nor challenged the idea of starting Taylor Home Remodeling, partly because I didn't ask her opinion. I was convinced of my ability to navigate alone in the business world. I needed no consultation from others in the field, and certainly none from my wife. Looking back it's easy to convict myself of insensitivity, but to do so paints an incomplete picture. I was always concerned about how my decisions would impact Jeannie and the kids, but to conduct my own business was normal and expected. Jeannie happily focused on raising our children and keeping the home fires burning. She didn't need my guidance to manage our family with excellence, and I felt grateful. On the other hand, I put food on the table and she felt secure. How I earned the money was up to me.

Our basement became an office, our garage a storehouse, and my first day in business I went out and bought a van. One of my earliest projects was at Greg's house, where I did everything myself—drywall, painting, ceiling, electrical. I hired no subcontractors, although Jeannie did help to carry drywall down the stairs! After many long days the project turned out great, and Greg eagerly publicized his home renovation, underpinning the small but impressive portfolio upon which I was determined to build. Yes, pun intended.

About a month later I hired Vic, a skilled carpenter with business experience. Before long we had multiple projects in motion. On two of them we lost our shirts, but our work was high quality, and word soon spread. More projects surfaced, and in our second year I moved the company office from my basement to a house in Camp Hill, where I successfully begged Jeannie to keep the books and complete a variety of administrative tasks. I also hired employees to take my place in the field, allowing me to focus on pursuing new projects in some of the area's most prominent neighborhoods.

A Word from Jeannie...

Full-time wife and mother? Fine by me.

I was content to stay home with the kids, happy we had not moved to Exton, and surprisingly at ease with Mark's business plan. This time he had an investor, a successful business owner, to cover start-up costs. And Greg was also a friend, willing and able to counsel my husband through the financial side of entrepreneurship.

Go to work for Mark? Not so fine by me.

I was seeing light at the end of the parenting tunnel. Our youngest child was about to start school. As a mom, freedom was near. I'd soon have days to myself, get things done around the house. But Mark didn't understand this. He viewed my freedom as a perfect opportunity to support his business. I reluctantly agreed to help him for a year. Only one year.

And felt as if I'd lost control of me.

By year four, with Jeannie still hanging on as my admin, Taylor Home Remodeling had established a favorable and enduring reputation. I had twelve men employed and a pipeline full of projects. I'd also joined a country club, which I absolutely loved.

Jeannie didn't care for club culture but appreciated the opportunity to take our kids swimming on hot summer days. And I did get her on the links a time or two, warned that a husband should never teach his wife to golf. Like any beginner, Jeannie hacked and sliced and added bold shades of color to her typically wholesome vocabulary! I stayed my distance, tried to keep a straight face, but our mutual rounds were very short lived.

From a business perspective, playing golf and lounging at the club were networking goldmines that led to big projects. The club also worked for me on a personal level, feeling privileged to rub shoulders with powerful people. My ego soared as movers and shakers praised my work and hired my services.

So, I bought out Greg's share in the company.

For me, the move symbolized achievement, a rite of passage to exclusive ownership and decision making. To put it bluntly: I'd proven myself successful and saw little value in continuing to receive Greg's counsel.

My business. My decisions. Period.

Vic disagreed. I approached him one morning to talk about the future of Taylor Home Remodeling, boasting about growth and big projects ahead. Rather than echo my enthusiasm, Vic just stared at me stoically, and said, "Are we making money? Let's be sure we're making money before taking another step."

In hindsight, we were not making money, only living on cash flow, but I lacked the wisdom to understand the difference and the patience to listen to anyone who did. Instead I felt indignant, offended by Vic's question. His construction company had ended in bankruptcy. He'd done things his way, and where did that lead? For days I seethed over Vic's lack of awareness. He just didn't understand what I was capable of achieving. Wasn't grasping my potential. Wasn't on board with my desire to swing for the fences. Taylor Home Remodeling was standing center stage in a spotlight of undeniable success. Who was Vic to challenge my leadership? I fired him three months later, filling his position with an employee well-versed in saying what I wanted to hear.

Around this time I also hired the services of an accountant, Dwayne, from whom I expected support and perhaps, when necessary, some legally creative reporting. We'd been friends for several years, met at the club, and I could think of no one better to chart my success and spin numbers in directions I wanted to head. Now, please understand: I still called the financial shots. Dwayne worked offsite, in his own office, and was tasked only with the preparation of our monthly and annual statements, a role I would have preferred to do myself if not for all the hours spent wooing new clients and managing projects. But so shifts the entrepreneurial landscape. Opportunity knocks and must be let in. Taylor Home Remodeling was rapidly expanding, and I had no choice but to fly in higher circles.

At first Dwayne seemed a perfect fit. I found our monthly meetings satisfying, at times invigorating, like brisk morning walks through a meadow of escalating profits. Until the day he hit me with a sobering truth: taxes due were twice what they should've been. Feeling mostly annoyed, I told him cash was tight and I had other bills to pay. But my excuses only stiffened his countenance, and I vividly remember when he looked me in the eye and said, "Mark, you need to know this is very serious. Your interest and penalties will double every month." His words were calm, consoling, spoken by a friend who cared as much about me as he did about my business.

Nevertheless, I played the role of a salesman—business is picking up, our margins should improve, we're cutting costs as we speak—but nothing softened him. Dwayne brushed off my jargon, asserting all the more that my tax situation was dangerous and required immediate resolution in the form of financial restraint. I heard him, understood his concern, and even felt some red flags waving in my heart. But in terms of moving forward, our perspectives varied widely. What Dwayne called a crisis I defined as a smudge on my otherwise healthy portfolio, and though noteworthy, this tax dilemma was no reason to pull tight the reigns of business growth. I'd climbed uphill before, dodged a few curves. I knew without question that boosting business meant bigger numbers, and bigger numbers meant debts could be paid.

I'll admit my conscience had been pricked, and somewhere inside I wanted to heed Dwayne's warning and pursue a more conventional, cost-cutting approach. But in my mind, Dwayne was a bean counter, not an operations guy. He didn't grasp the nuances of business management. Didn't see the bigger picture. My eyes were locked upon a business landscape as bright as it was wide, and no amount of debt, IRS or otherwise, was going to derail Taylor Home Remodeling. Therefore, like Vic, I fired Dwayne and replaced him with a "yes man" too green to see past the smoke I'd become adept at blowing.

For the next several years, Taylor Home Remodeling flourished, landing job after job and employing many people. We secured our place among the premier remodelers of central PA, and my ego, I must admit, expanded in proportion to business growth. Did tax debt remain an issue? Of course, but business was booming and I truly believed that the clouds overhead would eventually clear. I saw no need to worry employees, suppliers, or anyone else. Including my wife. I was up to my eyeballs in IRS debt, and Jeannie knew nothing about it. From my perspective, managing children and home was strenuous enough; she didn't need my stress, too. The clouds would clear.

I once told a local newspaper: When my ship begins to sink, there's always a sandbar to prevent it going under. Well, sandbars are projects, and our projects, as you know by now, were always first-class, attracting new clients and diverse opportunities. We once designed and constructed a 2500-square-foot kennel with grooming rooms and a puppy delivery ward. We also built a state-of-the-art sound studio which, according to the architect, was one of the nicest of its kind in Pennsylvania. And we always had several projects running concurrently.

Sounds like a roadmap to success, doesn't it? But here's the thing: Multiple projects are generally easy for employees, sub-contractors, and suppliers who have little at stake in the overall picture. They show up for work, get paid, and everything is well. My role as company owner was much more complicated. Our large projects produced high income, but they also required money to begin and complete and do everything in between. Money, money, money! Around every corner, after every step of every project, someone needed paid. My cash flow records looked like splattered paint. I lived in a constant cycle of employees needing paychecks to support their families, material suppliers threatening to close lines of credit, and banks demanding payments with compounding interest on the mammoth loans I'd somehow managed to take out. And let's not forget the IRS, quietly tightening its grip on my throat.

Behind the scenes, my head pounded, my stomach churned. Dwyane's prognosis had proven correct: when a cash-flow frenzy leads to missing tax payments, it's a sink hole, a disaster in the making. I saw it playing out exactly as predicted, and felt an insufferable weight upon my shoulders. But prideful me could see but one resolution: save face and fight. Anything else meant owning up to failure. No way...never... not Mark Taylor. I would overcome debt by growing the company, and carry alone the stress of doing so. I would preserve my image, protect my family, and continue to walk upon a stage of manicured fairways. Thanks to the art of smoke and mirrors.

Before I explain, let me remind you that my family had no clue I was in trouble with the IRS. You will not find greater integrity and sincerity beyond the hearts of Jeannie and our children. They are wonderful people, and about that there must be no misunderstanding. And though it may sound strange at this point in the story, those same qualities, even then, also simmered in me. It's true. My heart beat with the legacy of my family, my faith, my foundation...my father. Like him I desired to live a noble life while honoring others in the process, investing in the people of my community above its institutions. I longed to be a remarkable husband and father, but I was also determined to excel in business, and out of that drive, pride took root in me. It inflated and distorted my self-image. It directed me away from wise and caring individuals, pushed me toward desperate and deceptive measures to rescue a business I knew was imploding.

We were flush with big projects, yet I constantly lacked the cash to cover costs or pay taxes. Financial humps became mountains, which brought pressure to keep growing, which in turn brought new financial humps. And to really comprehend the anxiety of this cycle you must understand that running any business is difficult, even in the best of times. I needed to know and follow ever-changing federal, state, and local regulations, as well as rules and ordinances specific to my industry. Policies and procedures impacted everything, and they varied according to project scope and location. Furthermore, I faced myriad costs, and not only those related to projects. Everyone who worked for me received health insurance, liability insurance, and workman's compensation. These alone increased the cost of an employee by up to fifty percent. And let's not forget office supplies, equipment, maintenance, vehicles, lease payments. The list of expenses was a mile long. What else could I do but continue chasing profits?

The company needed money, my image was at stake, and profit was the answer to both. Increasing profits was the only way I knew to save my business and maintain dignity. I could grow and overcome, or pull back and fail, which for me was never an option.

Often robbing Peter to pay Paul, my business became a corporate example of living paycheck to paycheck, and I became adept at disguising it all. Week after week, I'd figure out ways to mask financial trouble and ironically take pride in the process, forming a bizarre fascination with this unsettling art form.

My most common tactic was ignoring the IRS, which is slow to respond while venders, subcontractors, and employees are not. Rather than pay taxes I'd use available cash to silence squeaking wheels, avoiding embarrassment, and averting harsh words from the people and companies I dealt with daily. Not to mention my clients, many of whom were wealthy, intolerant homeowners. Sometimes I paid taxes the following week, but late payments did nothing to offset interest and penalties, exactly as my former accountant had warned. Nevertheless, IRS agents kept their distance as I strung them along with relative ease, creating a sense of illusion, as if my tax debt might somehow be inconsequential. I knew better. I just cared more about my image and maintaining my business than I did about IRS threats.

The situation maddened me. Tax debt felt like a sleeping giant, growing larger by the day. I strived to conceal it, even from my family, because the solution for me was one contract away, and until then I refused to ruin my reputation. No confessing. No consulting. No restructuring. I'd come too far for any of that. I waited instead for a single silver bullet. All I needed was one more big job...just one more.

With my family and friends, I shared only the good stuff, and we had plenty of beautiful projects to boast about. From the outside looking in, Taylor Home Remodeling was admirable, and despite financial woes I remained genuinely pleased with and proud of the work we were doing. One project around this time really peaked Jeannie's interest. A father and daughter had leased an end unit in the shopping complex where my office was located. Their goal was to open a fitness center for females only, and they wanted me to help design and build the whole thing. I remember telling Jeannie and sensing her enthusiasm. Work soon began, the project turned out great, and Jeannie became one of the first ladies to join Momentum Female Fitness, where she worked out almost daily.

She also continued to help me administratively, though no longer employed by Taylor Home Remodeling. She'd gone to work instead as a special needs aide in our school district. Then, familiar with the building industry, she accepted the position of construction secretary for a massive high school renovation project. After that, she became project coordinator for an area construction company. Jeannie's consistent employment was a blessing—more than she realized—as I privately struggled to make ends meet.

I did my best to hide financial trouble from her and the kids, protecting them, convinced it was the noble thing to do. I wanted them to believe in the company and think of it only as a firm foundation in their lives. By the time my debt reached dangerous proportions, our kids were in high school, considering college, and preparing for their futures. They deserved the freedom to invest their mental energy in maturing toward adulthood, not worrying about Dad's business. Under no circumstances would I place upon their fragile young minds the financial stress of my company. Neither would I sacrifice my family's well-being to repair it. They had played no part in creating the problem. They would not suffer because of it.

My business. My decisions. Period.

This once victorious declaration now felt like a noose around my neck.

A Word from Jeannie...

"You must build this!" I said, literally jumping for joy.

Mark had just told me about plans for a new women's fitness club. He thought the idea seemed silly. Not me. I'd had my fill of gyms with sweaty men and judgmental atmospheres. I loved the females-only concept, and I felt eager for the opportunity to work out in a supportive environment with equipment and classes.

But I sure didn't expect to meet Jesus there.

When Momentum Female Fitness opened, I went almost every evening. It became my escape, my happy place, where stress melted and friendships developed. Two of those friends were also class instructors, and they greatly impacted my life. These ladies were not only super cool and passionate about fitness, they were enthusiastic about life in ways I'd never experienced. Oh, I'd lived through plenty of good times, but what they had was something different, something deep and sustaining. What they had, I discovered, was a relationship with Jesus. Not just at church, where I'd learned to worship God, but in a daily walk of Christian faith, a faith that somehow defined who they were and how they lived.

I didn't understand it, but I craved the faith these instructors had. Especially at this point in my life, when despite his efforts to hide them I knew about Mark's business woes. Not the specifics, but certainly the seriousness and urgency of them. I knew he sometimes didn't pay himself or brought home just enough to pay the mortgage. And I felt the pinch of our shrinking grocery budget, which allowed me just $100 to buy two-weeks-worth of groceries for our family of five, including home goods such as toilet paper, soap, shampoo, cleaning products...

But he absolutely had to pay employees, a vendor, or some loud-mouthed contractor. Had to sacrifice our cash flow to keep his people happy! Mark wasn't sharing details, but neither was he hiding or shielding me from the reality of hard times. I knew things were desperate when he asked me to co-sign a third loan against our mortgage.

"This one will help us get over the hump."

"Whatever," I said, signing his papers, walking away.

My heart sunk. Red flags waved.

The Collapse
CHAPTER FIVE

Taylor Home Remodeling had cracked beneath the surface, and my life was crumbling around it. I felt overtaken daily by a deep, nauseating awareness that my beloved business was in serious trouble. Worse, the health of my family hung in the balance. I'd made many attempts to right the ship. Taken out loans for no purpose other than boosting cash flow or paying my twenty-four employees. Desperately I waited for that one big project to make everything better, but day after day, hope dissipated, reality blurred. I felt as if I'd fallen off the stage I'd been privileged to grace, and resorted instead to lurking in catwalks, avoiding angry players as I tugged against the pull of closing curtains.

I remember nights at Joanie's basketball games, zoned out and staring at hundreds of people, wondering if they knew my situation. Did familiar people now tiptoe around me, smiling with compassion? Was playful banter meant to spare my emotions? I also wondered who among them had ever experienced my level of financial stress. Had anyone in that blaring gymnasium stood toe-to-toe with a disgruntled IRS? I could hardly watch a game, overcome by paranoia. I trusted no one, suspected everyone.

Unsure where else to turn, I thought of calling my parents, although I dreaded them knowing about the mess I'd made of Taylor Home Remodeling. I put off the call for days, and then one evening, lying in our basement, I forced myself to dial. They asked right away what was wrong.

"The business is in trouble," I said.

"By how much?"

I answered honestly, blaming circumstances, downplaying my responsibility. They calmly listened, expressed concern. When the call ended I sat in silence, my stomach tight, my face warmed by shame. Within minutes they called back. "We've decided to refinance our home, liquidate some money, do what we can."

I thanked them, tears welling. Talk about a dagger to the heart.

Despite my determination to withhold from Jeannie the details of our financial burden, I knew she'd grown wise to its severity, especially when I asked her to sign a third bank loan, after which we owed twice the value of our home. She knew how strapped for cash I'd become, and that my thoughts were always elsewhere—scattered, private, inaccessible. She respectfully criticized and challenged me, as would any spouse in her situation, but still she trusted me, helped me, and kept mothering our children without pressuring me to explain the jagged red handwriting etched upon our lives. She also stayed active in church. Myself, not so much.

Occasionally, depending on the weather, I'd join my family for a service. More often Sunday mornings were a cherished time to golf, soaking in the peace and solitude of time on the links. During our weekly phone calls, my mother always asked if I'd gone to church. I'd tell her the truth, which was usually no. Her responses were kind, encouraging, and always full of hope. She wanted her boy at church, and I totally understood that, but the relaxation of golfing simply meant too much. Mom's persistent questions never changed my behavior, but they touched my heart, helped me feel loved, and I'm glad she never stopped asking.

In time, Jeannie followed my lead, not golfing but missing more church than she attended. My poor example, however, was not entirely to blame. An unfortunate scandal had soured our opinion and diminished our attachment to the church we'd been attending. And to be completely transparent, the escalating tension provided a convenient excuse to pull up stakes. Other members hung in there, praying the church to greener pastures, but I was halfway out the door already and Jeannie's eyes had been opened to a fresher, more personal view of Christian faith by instructors at Momentum Female Fitness. I'd learned from Jeannie that these instructors attended a large church in the area. Beyond that I didn't ask, and she didn't offer much except to say one was a vocalist like me. But I perceived enough in her subtle remarks to know Jeannie saw in these instructors a vibrancy and joy, rooted in faith, that to her was unfamiliar, even as a practicing Christian.

A Word from Jeannie...

I was alone in church. Mark was golfing. Again!

The service was typical, with repetitive responses that made it easy to zone out or just go through the motions. And I found my eyes fixed upon a beautiful wooden cross above the alter. Then I looked around the sanctuary, and thought: Surely, there must be more than this.

I didn't mean to disrespect our church or the families in attendance, but the formality of the service just lacked something personal. I couldn't put my finger on exactly what was missing. It

> *was something I'd seen in my health club instructors, my former Oil City neighbors, occasionally elsewhere, but rarely in church.*
>
> *Why?*
>
> *What was I missing?*

For two more miserable years, I clung to the stern of my sinking ship, silencing the loudest critics while ignoring or avoiding those on the sidelines. My parents' loving gesture was not enough. Neither were the bank loans I'd somehow been granted. My slippery slope became steeper and sharper. My methods more desperate and convoluted. Endlessly I searched for new and bigger projects, turning over in my mind every conceivable fix. I even began talking with a business consultant, a small but humbling step in the right direction. But it was way too little and far too late.

Emotional pain and intolerable guilt crippled me, gutted my life of all that once defined Mark Taylor. What sleep I managed happened only alone, on the couch, in the wee hours of the morning. Despite taking prescription Ambien, I spent most nights writhing and wrestling with what-if scenarios nothing short of sheer terror, much worse than the nightmares that haunted my slumber. I felt physically sick, mentally imprisoned.

By this point, the children knew something was wrong. They observed my anxiety and troublesome nights. And by day their loving dad had become a ticking time bomb, with a fuse that ignited over anything. I remember when my son Jerry, a senior in high school, disobeyed me with attitude and I absolutely lost it. Screaming and shouting, I pinned him to the wall, my hand clutching his chin. The action startled both of us. Jerry ran out of the house, and I sat on the stairs and discovered I was shaking. When the reality of what happened finally washed over me, I found Jerry and apologized, but the damage had been done. To him and me. Numb, hollow, unable to focus, I chose to see a doctor.

The diagnosis: total nervous breakdown.

I left the doctor's office with a prescription for anti-anxiety pills, which I swiftly filled and started taking. Regardless, the next day at the club I experienced unprecedented paranoia, convinced the other members knew about my breakdown. "Mark Taylor's gone nuts!" I imagined them thinking or whispering out of earshot. "He's absolutely lost his marbles."

Insurmountable debt. Haunted by guilt. Terrified of failure.

Prescription medication. Severe depression.

Paranoia!

Perhaps I had lost my marbles. A matter of opinion, I suppose. The indisputable fact was that a wrecking ball had delivered a solid blow to the chest of my life. My business was collapsing, and as a man I felt demolished. In March of 2003, my consultant convinced me to meet with a bankruptcy lawyer. What followed were the four hardest days of my life.

Thursday

My consultant met me at the lawyer's office. I hoped the meeting might provide new direction, a chance to gain perspective and rescue my business. But in my heart of hearts I knew the ugly truth: Taylor Home Remodeling was stuck in the sand beneath an ocean of debt from which I'd never resurface. So much for my newspaper quote, years ago.

The meeting was brief and purposeful. The lawyer's remarks straight forward, tempered by wisdom and experience. And I'll never forget the moment he leaned my direction, elbowed his desk, and said, "Mark, missing just one payroll tax payment is a death blow to most companies. A reliable indicator that closing is the prudent course of action." I'd missed several payroll tax payments, which was worse than not paying personal taxes because I'd been neglecting employee withholdings, taking serious risks with other peoples' money. I knew then and there, in a moment of terrifying clarity, that Taylor Home Remodeling was dead in the water.

I drove home defeated, feeling like a quitter but knowing that was far from the truth. I'd poured my heart into the business, invested countless hours, assembled talented teams, respected my clients, and always insisted on top quality work. I'd just made some bad decisions, allowed pride to dissuade me from dealing with problems when reasonable solutions were still within reach. I'd worked my guts out trying to make ends meet, but with methods that only pulled me deeper in debt, as Taylor Home Remodeling slipped farther from my grasp. I wasn't a quitter, but I sure needed an escape.

For years, anxiety had choked me, robbed me of sleep, and suffocated moments that should have been savored, precious seasons that happen once in a lifetime. Oh, how it hounded me! Evenings and weekends. Alone or with others. Every minute of every day, business pressure devoured me and plagued my family. No more. It had to end. No more fighting back. No more standing eight counts. The time had come to stay down on the mat.

And tell my wife I'd lost everything.

When I got home that afternoon, Jeannie was busy at the kitchen table. I approached and stood stoic before her, still gripping my briefcase. Our eyes locked. I said only five words: "I can't do this anymore."

Her expression went blank...then soft...then stern. I remember staring at her face, searching, desperate to know what was rising within her. "Not now," she said, sliding a finger past the corner of her eye.

I knew instantly what she meant. We were well-established, almost empty nesters, about to embark on rediscovering our marriage, seeing our children finish college, spoiling some grandchildren. How could I falter at this stage of life?

I silently studied her wayward glances, the compression of her lips, the subtle shakes of her head, bracing myself for: You can't do this! What about the house, the cars, the kids! It's your daughter's senior year of high school! Don't you dare, Mark Taylor!

Instead she stood and calmly said, "We'll be okay."

I put down my briefcase just in time for her embrace.

For the rest of the day we discussed our next steps. Should we close the business immediately or ride out the week? When and how should we tell employees...clients...suppliers? Not to mention our family. Although greatly disappointed, Jeannie's clear thinking offset the cloudiness of mine, and she believed Taylor Home Remodeling had to end at once. She felt my mental well-being was too much at risk, even for one more day. I agreed, wanting no part of soldiering through another week, especially knowing what loomed ahead.

We ended cold turkey. All projects ceased.

That evening I felt numb, which proved beneficial for the disconcerting task of notifying employees. I called my sales rep first, then my second in command. Our conversations were short, matter-of-fact. I detected no anger, heard no harsh words. These guys were experienced businessmen who, despite their shock, understood and accepted my decision. I doubted other employees would respond so politely, but I never found out. My second in command made those calls on my behalf.

My day had ended. Along with my dream.

Friday

No need to wake up; I'd never fallen asleep. Only tossed and turned and agonized over what needed done, the worst of which was notifying clients. Taylor Home Remodeling had six projects underway, all too far along to turn back. I could arrange to finish one with pre-purchased materials. For the remaining five, however, my only option was to cut the clients loose and leave their projects unfinished, without so much as a dime to refund them.

By mid-morning I'd eaten nothing and downed several cups of coffee, worsening my fatigue-driven nausea. The house was silent and empty as I sat in my basement, staring at the phone on my desk. My fingers tapped my knee for what felt like an hour. Finally I dialed, brought the phone to my ear, where ring tones taunted like sadistic little drum rolls. RING... You're about to shatter the hopes of a family that trusted you. RING... Their home renovations will not be completed. RING... The money they've invested has all been—

"Hello."

I'd return a cordial greeting, then confess the bad news. "I've decided to close the business."

"But what about the money?"

"I'm sorry, there is no money."

"Are you kidding me?"

"I'm sorry."

"How will we finish our project?"

"I don't know."

From here, some were dumbfounded. Others chose to rant and rave. One even threatened to kill me. And yet, in the end, I felt a sense of relief. I'd been forthcoming, prevented anyone from hearing the news second hand, remained level headed under scathing criticism, and accepted the blame for all that transpired. Through the five hardest calls I'd ever made in my life, my character remained intact. And thank God for that; it was all I had left.

That afternoon I turned out the lights, laid on the couch, and did absolutely nothing. Depleted beyond measure, I searched for strength, ironically, by reflecting on a call I'd made that morning. The man on the other end—a client losing money and rocked by the news I'd delivered—asked how I was doing. He even asked about my family. Amid obvious shock and disappointment, this man expressed concern for me, the bad guy! And boy did I appreciate it. In the poignant darkness hovering over my life, this man had placed a shimmering star for which, to this day, I am thankful.

Saturday

Nearly forty-eight hours since my decision to close the business, loneliness had all but overtaken me. I knew a thousand people but had no true friends. Nobody to call or lean on. My parents lived in Florida, but I wasn't prepared to tell them anyway. At home, my family needed me strong or at least to appear so. They knew I'd been knocked down but didn't comprehend the true depths of my brokenness. For Jeannie and especially the kids, I tried to project stability as the world around them dramatically shifted. I'd created the mess. I would withstand the worst of it.

Before the locks changed, we went to my office to collect what we could. Jeannie's boss agreed to come with us, and I rode in his pick-up, thankful for his soft and consoling remarks. Jeannie followed in our Ford Explorer. We parked behind the building to avoid irate clients, but discovered in the office something much more disturbing: employees in the act of stealing equipment to offset the money they wouldn't be paid. I ordered them to stop, and though tension hung thick and some vulgar words flew, they left without incident. Afterward, Jeannie and I boxed up surprisingly little—some personal items, incorporation documents, some business records. Then we turned and walked away from life as we knew it.

And for me, we couldn't move fast enough.

Now, you might think that sounds hasty or overly fatalistic, but that's how I felt at this point in the process. Run away! Bury your head! Let the chips fall where they may! But to do so was impossible. Sure, we drove away from the office and never returned, but you can't simply drive away from failure. Riding home in that truck, I felt competing measures of shame, rage, and depression. None of which I felt free to express, even if I'd wanted to. Instead, behind forced smiles and false bravado, I shot the breeze with Jeannie's boss, stuffing my pain to the sound of his well-intentioned platitudes.

Run away! Bury your head!

If only I could have.

Sunday

In no mood for people, I wanted nothing more than to turn our house into a cave of seclusion, a place to wallow in my emotional hangover. I'd agreed, however, as president of the athletic booster foundation, to emcee my daughter's high school basketball banquet. Joanie, a senior, wasted no time pleading for Daddy (the name she still calls me) to stay the course: "You really need to do it! This is my last sports banquet and I want you to be there."

Anxiety gripped me almost to the point of paralysis. A leadership role at a public event was the last thing I needed so soon after closing the business. All afternoon I battled irrational thoughts beyond the evening's agenda. Could I ever show my face in public again? Would every outing be a covert operation to avoid people I'd hurt, employees out to get me, and former clients with axes to grind? Moreover, what about the people who still treated me well? Would I label them phonies, doubt their true opinions? *Mark Taylor, great to see you... You big jerk! Failure! Crook!*

The evening arrived much too quickly, and the bustle of getting ready only further unnerved me. Prepared remarks were folded neatly in my jacket, and they would be easy to deliver. The words I feared most—those which might spring forth unfiltered at the mention of my business—were much less organized. They felt volatile, tied strictly to emotion. Who knew what I might say if the closing came up? I hoped it wouldn't, but the odds were definitely not in my favor.

The banquet ambience was typical: cloth-covered tables set with ten or twelve chairs; reserved spaces near the front; pitchers of water; baskets of buns; an occasional burst of nervous teenage laughter to pierce the low murmur of parents conversing.

Before we'd even found our seats, I saw a former client approaching. "Hey, it's been a while. How are you?" I said, forcing a name to surface, extending a hand she didn't take.

"My brother-in-law trusted you. I recommended you. How could you let this happen?"

And so it began. Everything I feared stood before me. The whole room seemed to watch as I choked down every defensive word on my tongue, slipped my hands in my pockets, and said, "I'm sorry."

"Not good enough. He's in the middle of a job, house torn apart, and screwed out of the money he's invested! What are you going to do about it?"

"There's nothing more I can do. Again, I'm very sorry."

She glared at me a few seconds longer, and then walked away as I hurried to a table, feeling conspicuous, like the brunt of all jokes in a room full of happy, chatty people. It was all I could do not to leave.

As the evening continued, I somehow managed to put on a smile and steer conversations away from myself. Stepping to the podium, I was warmly greeted and felt momentarily whole. I called the players forward, teased those I knew well, honored their coaches, and recapped special moments. I stepped away with a sense of relief, perhaps even healing. Until I saw her approaching.

Another former client, her face stern, her eyes piercing mine. She said, "I cannot believe you had the audacity to stand on that stage after what you've done."

I wanted to shoot back, defend myself and my right to emcee this banquet. But I relented, took the punch, and sheepishly offered the words I'd said over and over since Thursday: "I'm sorry."

"You said it," she countered, turning away.

I gathered my family and went home.

Dust and Rubble

CHAPTER SIX

When Taylor Home Remodeling closed, Jerry and Joanie still lived at home and therefore heard the news immediately. Other family members had not, and I firmly believed they deserved to find out about the closing from me. So, that's how I began the next week.

I called my parents first, got them both on the line, and kept them nervously waiting through an awkward few seconds. The words I'd intended to speak felt lodged in my throat as embarrassment stiffened me, tightened my jaw. This was not a plea for help. I'd officially failed.

"Bad news," I eventually said. "I've decided to close the business."

Prolonged silence.

"What does that mean?" my mother asked.

"I've lost it all. We're ending the business. Declaring bankruptcy."

Mom asked a few more questions, but Dad said nothing, his silence only worsening my shame. I'd worked so hard to prove myself to him, to make my father proud, and he'd refinanced his home to help lift me out of debt.

"I'll find a way to pay you back," I said, unprompted.

"We understand," my mom said. "That's the least of our concerns."

Still, my father said nothing.

Our conversation fizzled, then ended, and fear of what they said afterward haunted me for months. Later that day, I called my brother

Scott. His response was caring and supportive. My daughter Jamie was also understanding and not overly surprised. After graduating college, before joining a prominent accounting firm, she'd kept the books at Taylor Home Remodeling. She'd caught glimpses of my unbalanced finances, seen the stress I was under, and like Jerry and Joanie, she knew running a company was only what I did, not who I was. The kids grieved the loss, but mostly they wanted me well.

Not so for many in the community.

I dreaded going anywhere I might encounter people, especially the grocery store. But with time on my hands and Jeannie fully employed, shopping seemed the least I could do. Peering down each aisle, I'd slip in only when the coast was clear, hoping my fedora and fake mustache stayed in place. Okay, I'm joking about the disguise! But I did proceed with caution, ducking all familiar faces, unsure who might lash out. I also had no interest in answering questions about how I was doing. My mission was to stock the cart, pay the bill, and retreat.

It didn't take long for news to reach the country club, where I knew the networking (gossip) that once filled my project pipeline would now conspire against me. Resignation was in order, but I couldn't bear the shame of submitting it in person. Instead I wrote a letter, fumbling for words to end my privileged membership. The club meant the world to me. It was my haven, my escape. At the club I breathed easier, forgot about troubles, savored pristine links and gourmet cuisine. To resign was to amputate a part of myself.

Perhaps you're questioning how business bankruptcy causes personal hardship. For those inexperienced with bankruptcy, which I pray includes you, the process can certainly be confusing. Here's a snapshot: Filing Chapter 13 (business) bankruptcy is a protective measure, something I did almost immediately after closing Taylor Home Remodeling. At that time, my business was indebted to numerous suppliers, clients, banks, and other entities. If the news had reached them, the demand for money would have soon turned ugly. Bankruptcy protected me from these obligations. Financial disputes over my failed business became the responsibility of my bankruptcy attorney.

Sounds nice, doesn't it? But I'll caution you not to read a hint of joy into this explanation. Relief, yes, but not happiness. A person filing business bankruptcy does not simply wipe his brow and casually move forward to another endeavor. Bankruptcy is neither a pleasant escape nor the business equivalent of a childhood do-over. To the contrary, it's nothing short of raw failure, made formal and public. It causes anger, grief, and insufferable shame. Its personal impact cannot be overstated.

For a company owner, personal finances intertwine with business. It's normal, commonplace, practically unavoidable. For instance, I borrowed money for Taylor Home Remodeling by using my house as collateral. I started lines of credit and hired contractors with my personal signature endorsing each commitment. Our Ford Explorer was paid for by the company, as was half of our mortgage. I used personal credit cards to pay business expenses, racking up huge amounts of debt. After many years in business, I'd gotten my personal finances so interconnected with Taylor Home Remodeling that distinguishing between them seemed nearly impossible. We needed business to thrive so we could survive. But I'd blown it. No more business. No more income. And Jeannie's job paid too little to offset the loss.

Because of the multiple times I'd borrowed against our house, our mortgage payments were enormous. My credit card debt was also severe, and I drove an SUV I could no longer pay for. We struggled with bills, living expenses, and missed many loan payments, quickly compounding the problem. As desperation set in, everything unnecessary had to be sacrificed, including things that mattered dearly to Jeannie, like her health club membership. Bankruptcy had protected us from conflict, but my family was nevertheless at risk of financial ruin. A fate I felt determined to avoid.

A Word from Jeannie...

From the day we closed the business, things became different. An obvious statement, I know, but I'm talking scary different, the kind of change that's hard to understand unless you've lived it. Bankruptcy felt like a dirty word stamped upon my forehead. And like my husband-turned-hermit, I avoided people as much as possible, thinking everyone knew my world was collapsing. They didn't, of course, but I imagined it so, which made me self-conscious in almost any setting. Walking the dog, school events, shopping, even at church, I sensed eyes upon me. Who really knew didn't seem to matter much; my emotions were aligned with irrational perception, and I felt almost as paranoid as Mark. Almost.

Financially, we were in crisis. The government routinely checked our accounts, entitled to whatever money it found there. Everything had to be purchased with the little bit of cash we had on hand, no exceptions. Head down, hoping not to be noticed, I'd meticulously calculate every item in my cart. So frustrating and humiliating! I quickly learned the heartbreak of limiting purchases to only what we needed, I mean really needed. We lived leaner than I'd ever thought possible, afraid to splurge on cookies or brand name coffee.

But Mark felt certain we would not lose the house.

I prayed he was correct, the thought of it more than my heart could bear.

A skilled salesman, I felt fully capable of schmoozing my way back to life as we knew it, including country club membership. That's why I did my best to save face. For example, my outstanding balance at the club (from hosting my parents' fiftieth anniversary party) could have been absolved by my bankruptcy, but I chose to pay it off, little by little, over several years. I did the same with some hefty dental bills, because our dentist was a friend I'd played golf with at the club. He'd hired Taylor Home Remodeling to do a project at his house, and he was also a hero to two of our kids. Here's the quick version: Middle school gym class, Jerry got a tooth knocked out, root and all. I was called to the gruesome scene where I helped coordinate medical attention, which of course included a trip to the dentist. Then, within minutes of returning to my office, the elementary school called. I answered with a joke about how I'd just dealt with Jerry's tooth trauma. Unamused, the secretary instructed me to sit, and told me Joanie had broken some teeth playing basketball. Two in one day! Our dentist repaired both smiles with expertise and compassion.

The favorable opinions of country club members mattered more to me than absolving every debt. Why? Because Mark Taylor was down but not out. The beast of burden was behind me, and from that fact alone I drew a sense of relief. I'd made the gut-wrenching calls, taken my lumps, and despite the pain of losing my business, or maybe because of it, my drive to succeed had found firm footing. Don't misunderstand: I was in deep financial trouble, still struggling with guilt, shame, and depression. And thoughts of how it all happened still bothered me. But as days clicked by and a new normal took shape, I slipped back to a pattern of stuffing my pain and operating publicly as if things were fine, always playing the salesman. My default setting was to market myself, and more than ever I had to open the right doors, impress the right people. I'd promised Jeannie we would not lose our home. And we wouldn't. Not on my watch.

Privately, sure, I'd let the rough side drag—sitting in seclusion, often in the basement. I ate very little as I struggled with anger and depression. I failed to sleep, and throughout the night, whether staring at walls or pretending to watch television, thoughts of failure bombarded my mind. But so did thoughts of redemption, pangs of determination to restore my reputation and once again prove—to family, colleagues, clients, and the world—my competency, my proficiency, and my dedication to excellence. I'd begin, much to my dismay, by peddling lighting supplies.

"Hello, my name is Mark Taylor. May I please speak to the person responsible for the purchase of your lighting supplies?" Although quirky, my go-to line was very effective. Most people stared back, speechless, as if I'd gone crazy, which opened doors to conversation and my well-polished pitch. Sure, this job felt pathetic, a waste of my talent. I'd been the owner and president of a premier remodeling company. I'd held leadership positions with two of the region's largest home builders. Long term, chasing door-to-door sales was completely unacceptable, but it met short-term needs at a time when everything I owned felt jeopardized.

Around this time my parents visited from Florida, and Dad finally spoke about the business closing. We were alone in the house and running out of things to talk about. "Mark," he began. "I've just gotta ask. How did this happen?"

There it was, bare and hovering between us.

I stumbled through a litany of shallow excuses: didn't make money; the well just ran dry; bad decisions; personnel issues; yadda, yadda. In the presence of my father, every line felt sad, but what angered me most was his apparent lack of empathy. He cared about my pain but seemed unable to grasp what had led to it. Remember: Dad was a lifelong corporate man, a cog in a system. He'd never felt the pressure or navigated the challenges of owning a business. As I walked him through the reasons behind my bankruptcy, he listened respectfully but never quite seemed to understand. Not really. And I started to wonder if he thought himself superior, as if he'd built a proper career, done things correctly, while I chased dreams and fell flat on my face. I hated feeling this way about Dad, and yet the longer I talked the more defensive I became. I'd provided sufficient, acceptable answers, and I would not be judged by a man who'd never walked in entrepreneurial shoes.

Later, I cried about disappointing Dad and feeling such indignation. Whether he fully understood my situation did not matter. Sharing life with him was always important, validating, the one thing that seemed to solidify the reality of anything significant. I suppose in every man lives the boy he used to be, pursuing warmth and praise from a loving father. In this world or the next.

I resigned from lighting sales to accept a position as project manager for an area contractor. Back in my world, I wasted no time spewing expertise at all who would listen. In my mind, they were lucky to have me. I saw operational flaws and untapped markets, brashly encouraged rapid growth and bigger spending. At home, money remained a major problem, missing payments, living week-to-week. But this new job seemed a step in the right direction, a rung on the proper ladder. Mark Taylor was climbing again…but about to be knocked right back down.

I received Jeannie's call while waiting in a barber shop. Fear in her voice, she said, "Mark, there's a tow truck in the cul-de-sac, taking our car." Now, by car she meant Ford Explorer Limited, fully-loaded and in excellent condition. At first I panicked, skin warming with rage, until reality threw a wet blanket around me. Losing the Explorer was just another gut punch for mistakes I'd made. All I could do was let it go, take the lump. I tried to calm Jeannie, consider our options, but there was nothing we could do.

Hanging up, I imagined the scene and what our neighbors must be thinking. How embarrassing for Jeannie. When and where would this madness end? I had another decent job, but like Eeyore's cloud, depression hovered overhead. Our financial picture was perilous, a race against time, of which I had little. Freshly trimmed, I raced back to work in my company car.

I'd lost our vehicle. I would not lose our house.

A Word from Jeannie...

I noticed a tow truck approaching our cul-de-sac, and wondered which neighbor had car trouble. Until it stopped at our house.

From an upstairs bedroom, I watched, confused, expecting the driver to come to our door. Instead he referenced a clipboard, checked our Ford's VIN, and started prepping to tow it. Heart pounding, I called Mark immediately, but his response was lame, like, "Just let it go. There's nothing we can do."

Really? My knight in shining armor.

Disappointed in Mark and growing madder by the second, I rehearsed in my mind what the neighbors must be thinking, or how I could spin the whole situation. Losing our vehicle infuriated me, made me feel almost sick, especially since I'd just landed a job near Hershey. How was I supposed to get to work? Fortunately, a nearby co-worker let me ride with her, though she was none too happy about it. Talk about awkward.

> *It took nearly a month for Mark and me to scrounge enough money for a dippy used car, which, pardon the expression, totally sucked! We were nearing our golden years.*
>
> *Life wasn't supposed to turn out this way.*

Within a year I accepted the position of regional manager for a major home builder. They assigned to me complete responsibility for three housing developments in the city of York, south of Harrisburg. The commute was a bear, but the job a promotion, a necessary step in my quest for self-preservation. My team and I handled everything, and the market was crazy. Houses sold in such rapid succession we hardly had time to run utility lines. The frantic pace of my marathon days led to strained relationships, especially with my boss, and a level of anxiety I hadn't experienced since the fateful last days of Taylor Home Remodeling.

As time went on and the market showed no signs of slowing, my relationship with my boss deteriorated further. Stressed beyond measure, I felt little support and was reminded almost daily that corporate bonuses hinged upon my team's ability to settle enough houses before year end. Fortunately my salespeople and managers were excellent, up to the task of meeting corporate demands in a burgeoning market. We settled eighteen different homes in the fourth quarter alone. Under intense pressure, we rose to the occasion, and I felt proud of myself and my team. Anxiety, however, continued taking its toll.

Early in the new year, my boss invited me to have lunch and discuss the general status of my communities, which probably meant berating me for unresolved issues. Well, one of those issues was a shower door problem that had surfaced several times. Knowing this situation would likely be part of our lunchtime conversation, I took the initiative to stop by that house, touch base with the repair technicians, and provide my boss with real time information. The stop took longer than expected, so as soon as I sat down in my car to leave, I called to tell him I'd been held up at the client. And he unloaded: "I can't believe you'd turn down the opportunity to have lunch with your VP!" Among other choice words and phrases. I said nothing in response. Just hung up the phone and sat shaking in my car, enraged. I'd poured blood, sweat, and tears into this company. Worse, my boss considered himself more important than our clients.

Next thing I knew I was at home with Jeannie, unsure how I'd gotten there. Anxiety had me in a stupor, dazed and disoriented. I allegedly curled up on the couch, unresponsive, which scared Jeannie enough to drive me to the hospital. I say "allegedly" tongue in cheek because, years later, when discussing this episode as part of the book-writing process, I had no recollection of it. Jeannie repeatedly insisted, as I listened in astonishment, that she had in fact coaxed me from the couch and taken me to the emergency room. I literally said, "Okay, Honey. If you say so!" We all shared a good laugh, although the story was sobering.

Jeannie's concern was that I might be suicidal. Thankfully my evaluation indicated otherwise. The doc sent me home with orders to see a therapist and take time off work, which is something I do remember. I called my office that night to inform them I would not be in for a week, which I spent soul searching, rationalizing, torn between my health, my future, and the well-being of my family. This company was killing me, my boss was a jerk among jerks, but we needed the money and I desperately wanted to leverage this position toward rebuilding my career. I toughened my resolve, returned the next Monday.

That morning I was fired.

A Word from Jeannie...

Our conversation felt strange. This just wasn't my Mark.

He'd called mid-afternoon with news he was on the way home. He also shared some of his boss's insensitive comments, which I knew he'd grown accustomed to hearing. But these remarks seemed especially rude, and I could hear how deeply they'd cut my husband.

Mark's stress was always sky high, and he'd already experienced anxiety attacks, in my opinion. But talking to him this day, I sensed in my heart he'd been pushed too far and that something was seriously wrong. I asked if he was okay. He said he didn't know. I told him to pull over. He refused, claiming to be almost home.

I sat near the front window, awaiting his arrival. A short time later, he pulled in the drive and walked right in the house. I knew his mental condition was especially bad when he laid on the couch, curling himself into a fetal position. I tried to talk about what happened at work, but he wouldn't communicate. He only laid there motionless, eyes glazed over. And my heart began to pound. I shared my fear with Mark and insisted he go to the emergency room. Thankfully, he complied, although today he has no recollection of doing so.

When we arrived at the hospital, medical staff monitored Mark's vitals and performed routine checks before directing us to meet

> *with a psychiatrist. I silently stood by as Mark slumped in a chair, staring at the floor, answering questions. After each one, he hesitated, gathering thoughts to the best of his ability. I eagerly awaited the question that mattered most to me: Are you feeling suicidal? When the doctor finally asked it, Mark instantly said no, without any hesitation, and I felt so relieved! When the evaluation ended we were given information about local psychiatrists. The doctor recommended Mark start seeing one ASAP.*
>
> *Once home, Mark curled up on the couch again.*
>
> *I sat near him, unsure what just happened or what to do next.*

Being fired had forced my hand. Jeannie and I were in crisis, and I needed income from anyone ready and willing to hire me. I accepted a position at Engle Business Systems, where I went to work as a business accounting software consultant. Yes, you read that correctly; I'd talked them into hiring a bankrupt businessman to work as an accounting software consultant. Snake oil, anyone? Adding to the irony, I found myself back in a cubicle. Whenever possible, however, I'd leave the office and travel to clients. I hated discussing computer-based accounting by phone. Quite honestly I wasn't that smart!

Although certainly not working in my preferred occupation, I learned a lot as an accounting software consultant, and the income helped us limp along. For months, we scraped by. And then we didn't. Growing deeply concerned, I messaged our attorney. He returned the call as I sat in my car, finishing lunch at McDonald's. I told him everything, explaining that despite our hard work we were drowning financially, missing mortgage payments, unable to afford essential items. He listened respectfully, then gave it to me straight: "Mark, there's only one thing left to do. File personal bankruptcy and stop paying the mortgage. You'll skate by a few months until foreclosure." His direct advice was a kick to the gut, and I hoped my Big Mac would stay down. Today was a day I'd thought might come but hoped beyond hope it would not. Foreclosure became reality. My years of effort were cut off at the knees. Our home would be lost.

And I had to tell Jeannie.

I withheld the news from her until the subject of our house came up naturally, about a week later, as we sat together in the living room. She responded with frustration but not surprise; she'd seen the signs, perceived this death blow approaching. Nevertheless, tears fell from her eyes. Mine, too. Wounded, confused, I swallowed many wrong words before they formed on my tongue. Then I turned and walked away from the woman who'd trusted me. But what more could I say? I'd promised better days for years. Never delivered. At least I could provide her with some time alone to grieve.

Mark Taylor had failed again.

A Word from Jeannie...

I knew foreclosure was a real possibility, but to hear it from Mark was big-time devastating.

I did take time for a sobbing cry, but afterward I hurt deeply for him. Telling me about the loss of our twenty-year home, our supposed-to-be-forever home, was one of the hardest things he had to face in the aftermath of losing his business. I wouldn't let him bear the pain alone.

I feared for my husband's mental stability, and the last thing I wanted was to come across mad or put the blame all on him. I just couldn't do it. I loved him too much. We were in this thing together, for better or worse, for richer or poorer, in sickness and in health. We'd made those vows before our pastor, family, friends, and most importantly God. I was determined to honor and uphold them. But believe me, I did have my moments!

One day around this time, before the start of a class at Momentum Female Fitness, my instructor tapped me on the shoulder and informed me she'd be singing that Sunday in her church, Christian Life Assembly (CLA), if I'd like to attend. Well, of course I did. Mark even came with me, and we loved our experience in this large church. My instructor's solo was outstanding, and the music overall felt modern and moving. People were friendly, the facility was beautiful, and the sermon was personal, applicable, and relevant to the realities of everyday life.

Mark and I attended CLA somewhat regularly after this weekend, and despite his personal struggles, Mark chose to involve himself in ministry, as did I, making wonderful friends who invested in my life at a time when everything was falling apart. I eventually told my fitness instructor about the Sunday, years earlier, when I'd stared at the cross in our former church and felt moved to seek more of Jesus. In response she talked about her reluctance to share the dates when she'll be singing and said why she'd told me was a mystery to her.

But God knew why. His timing had been perfect.

Days later, Jeannie and I filed for Chapter 7 bankruptcy. Our attorney did the paper work, completed all the forms. We simply signed and initialed through the process. Later we appeared in a storm-gray courtroom, taking turns before a judge. My heart hit the floor when Jeannie stood at the bench. It was normal procedure, something we'd expected, but watching my dear wife answer questions under oath about the mess I'd made was agonizing, simply unbearable. Afterward, riding down the courthouse elevator, our attorney looked at Jeannie and smugly told her we were going to lose our house. I wanted to punch him almost as much as myself. We drove home in silence in our crappy used car, and I couldn't help but wonder why Jeannie even stayed with me.

Rarely had I concerned myself with thoughts of losing Jeannie, which in hindsight I consider my biggest risk of all. Words cannot express how shattering it would have been to lose her, but in the thick of my pride and unrelenting pain, I invested little in preserving our marriage. Honestly, bless her heart, Jeannie didn't complain much. Although she had every right to unload on me daily, she consistently kept her peace. Now and again she made clear this was not what she expected at this stage in life, but then I'd feel picked on, beaten down by my own wife. I'd lost my business. Smeared my reputation. I was the victim, not her, and she was supposed to feel sorry for me. We'd argue, drop it, move on without resolve. In my heart I understood the tremendous loss Jeannie was experiencing. The anger. The disappointment and fear. Nevertheless, I tuned out her pain because to me it was a hinderance, a distraction to my need to get up and move on.

I had no interest in consolation, no desire for heartfelt talks about life and lessons and where to go from here. I'd suffered enough and wanted only to reestablish my life. What I needed, what we needed, was a big fat break, a golden opportunity to set things right. I'd convinced myself Jeannie understood this and would therefore pardon my flaws in marriage. I assumed she wanted my success as badly as I did. I thought she considered my determination admirable, even mutually beneficial. In my victory, she would heal. In my victory, she would find renewed hope.

In my victory... God forgive me.

When explaining home foreclosure, our attorney had informed us that a recurring docket of Sherriff Sale houses was inserted monthly into newspapers, and once our home listed we'd be served eviction papers within thirty days. Every month I'd force myself to open that dreaded insert. We survived only a few.

When our address appeared, it was a shot to the heart. Our beloved home, our hall of memories, publicly foreclosed and for sale in a real estate thrift store. That very week we saw cars trolling the cul-de-sac, evaluating our house. Each creeping vehicle brought tears to our eyes and an ache to our hearts, but with little left to say we simply gave each other space as we boxed our possessions. To pack up our home was to pack up our lives, and the pain was intense, almost tangible. The end was near. We were living out our final days at home, about to walk away from Jeannie's wonderful kitchen, the picture window where every December our Christmas tree stood, the cathedral ceilings, the children's rooms, and the porch where their pennies smiled up from the floor.

Never had my failure in business hit harder.

But you must understand also that to me foreclosure was just another boot to the ribs of one very dead horse. I desperately wanted to save our house, but when I could not, the loss felt matter-of-fact. It hurt very much, but by then I'd learned to deal with pain mechanically. Not on purpose. I wasn't behaving like some brush-burned kid on the playground of life, gritting my teeth, refusing to cry. My take-a-punch mentality was deeper, more authentic. It reflected where I'd been and where life had deposited me. Since closing the business I'd pulled my head above water, felt glimmers of hope, but life still felt like a perpetual smear of my face in the soiled remains of my failure. I'd therefore conditioned myself to turn off my pain, throw ice on my sadness, and push myself forward. Toughen up and move on became the mantra of my never-ending quest to win again.

Foreclosure. Eviction. Toughen up and move on.

A few days later, the sun setting, I noticed the Sheriff pulling into our drive. I opened the front door before he had time to knock. He smiled. I did not. And we exchanged no pleasantries. I wasn't angry, only eager to get the formality behind me. He handed me the papers, and said, "Please don't be upset. These are documents I need to serve you. Contact your attorney. I hope things work out."

I thanked the Sheriff, closed the door, and tossed the papers on a table. I knew Jeannie was nearby, aware of what had just happened, but I provided no hugs, expressed no emotions. I only pondered the situation, alone and defeated, determined to fix my broken world. I would find the right psychiatrist, the right anti-depressant, the right connections, the perfect job. I'd do whatever I needed to reestablish myself.

Until then we'd simply rent a townhouse.

A Word from Jeannie...

My heart sank as I watched their exchange.

The sheriff was kind, respectful, but Mark said almost nothing. As the door closed he put down the papers and returned to the task of boxing up our lives. He knew I'd been watching. And it hurt to be ignored.

I knew this day was coming but had prayed it might not, hoping God would fix things or wake me from the nightmare. But that wasn't His plan. It wasn't Mark's either, and yet here we were, packing up the rooms where I'd laughed, loved, and nurtured; where I'd cooked, cleaned, and decorated; where I'd snuggled, disciplined, bandaged, comforted, listened to and guided my three precious children; and where I'd prayed in the glow of soft sunsets and candles, so thankful for the life I'd been given.

To me, these walls had absorbed our memories, soaked in our emotions, but they would soon surround a different family. New children would inhabit the rooms where mine had played, studied, and hid beneath covers on dark stormy nights. A new mom would serve meals and fold laundry in my kitchen, hang clothes in my closets, and sip tea on my porch, questioning or maybe even chiseling away the three cherished pennies embedded there.

Mark seemed almost eager to move, to turn the page and run away from the pain he felt responsible for causing. I understood his point of view, but I also hated it. We were losing and grieving together. He wasn't the only one feeling pressure. I was in a new job, learning new software, and driving around in a crappy used car! His determination to get back in the game was no excuse to minimize this traumatic loss. Our home of twenty years, our forever home, was being ripped away from us, my heart along with it.

Life sure isn't fair.

Our last night at home, I wrote a prayer. Simple words from a broken heart. Here it is, original and unpolished:

Dear God,

Today is Friday, November 17, 2006. It was a good day! Lord, I come to you with great sadness in my heart. This is my last night here in my home. I'm having a hard time saying goodbye. Lord, we've been here for 20 years. I have to accept this, and understand that you have plans for my life. God, I pray you lead me and guide me through that righteous path. I surrender my heart and soul to you. Guide me, lead me, show me your ways. Lord, even though I feel sadness, this has made me grow. Sometimes we have to be put through a fire in order to see the light. Thank you, Lord, for all you have done for me. I am thankful for my husband, children, and all of our family who have been so supportive of us. I am thankful for ways that the church has been supportive. I give PRAISE to you Lord!

Thanks for listening,

Amen.

New Beginnings
CHAPTER SEVEN

We chose an end-unit townhouse in a secluded community. Our tiny yard ran adjacent to a patch of woods, but it was hardly comparable to our cul-de-sac serenity. Our biggest concern was making the move. Everything was packed, but we had way too much for our small car, and hiring movers was out of the question. Even renting a truck would strain our meager finances.

That week at church choir rehearsal, behind practiced smiles and guarded small talk, I carried this burden. And much to my surprise, I shared it while chatting with a man I barely knew. I vaguely explained that Jeannie and I needed to move in a hurry and under tense circumstances. To this day I don't know why I caved and got personal, but I'll never forget his response. In just hours, this guy arranged a small group of people to move us into the townhouse. They wanted no compensation, only to serve a new family in their church. I left that night with a strange blend of thoughts and feelings. Though deeply grateful, I felt also confused and even slightly uncomfortable. Their eagerness to help me, a near stranger, made me uneasy, and yet it brought hope and a feeling of peace. At the risk of sounding sappy, I honestly felt loved.

That weekend we moved from our forever home, one of the saddest events in my life. But having help from church families was truly a blessing. The group moved our stuff and cared for us. They filled our whole day with compassion, humor, and a deeply moving sense (pun intended) that their desire to love us was honest and sincere. I didn't understand that mindset, but I clearly sensed in these people what Jeannie had discovered in her health club instructors—a personal relationship with Jesus Christ. I also realized that day, not with clarity so much as a churning intuition, that my heart was in the wrong place. I'd made our new church about me, a place to rebuild myself. I wanted God to provide what I thought I needed. Joining the choir and acting in dramas harkened back to glory days, allowed me to show off my talents. My church inroads had been mostly selfish paths, and the hearts of these movers had exposed my flawed agenda.

That night I silently prayed before drifting off to a restful night's sleep—a rare and cherished commodity. When I woke up the next morning, I felt at peace for the first time in ages. The foreclosure was behind me, another box checked on my journey back to life as it should be. And for now it seemed God had my back.

The first week in our townhouse, I traveled for business. Jeannie, however, went to clean our "true" home and deal with a few outstanding details. For her this was vital. More than memories, our former house was an extension of us, and she wasn't about to be labeled a slob. We were leaving behind an impression of our family, and her honor as a homemaker was somehow at stake.

I, on the other hand, missed our home but felt energized by the townhouse. No kidding. Being away from things I could no longer afford felt freeing. A new house, no matter the size, was a new beginning, and for me that bred optimism. Things were looking up. We wouldn't even have been able to rent the townhouse if not for a stroke of good fortune. Remember, our credit was horrendous! But at the time of our foreclosure, this townhouse community just happened to be running a two-month special: no credit check, special financing. The stars were certainly aligning.

Between Jeannie's employment and my job at Engle Business Systems, we brought in enough to make ends meet and chip away debts. Boxes got unpacked, our tiny kitchen got organized, and slowly but surely life took on a new normal. Even my working relationships felt altered.

Cory was a talented colleague and, as fate would have it, an avid golfer. As our friendship grew, we soon took to spending evenings shanking drives on courses that were...well...not exactly country club status. The funny thing was I stopped caring, even found myself attracted to the simplicity of unpretentious living. Cory was nothing like the man I used to be, but he was authentic, and that I found very appealing. His car was a late model something or other, with a sticker that read: Drive a Titleist! He lived every day as a down-to-earth guy, full of hope and joy. In Cory I discovered the impressiveness of humility, which he openly attributed to faith in Jesus Christ.

My manager, Patrick, one of the most brilliant men I know, was also a Christian. One day he asked about my situation outside of work. He already knew the basic details and seemed to truly care how I was doing. So, I took a risk and talked about the pain of losing in life. Afterward, Patrick prayed. Then he looked in my eyes and said, "Mark, Jesus loves you, this I know, for the Bible tells me so." Weird and corny but totally sincere, his words made an impact on my life. That night I shared them with Jeannie, who affixed them via Post-it to her bedroom mirror, where they remain to this day.

In 2007, Engle Business struggled, and I was laid off. It was difficult to leave my colleagues, especially Cory and Patrick, but I also wondered whether this was God's timing and a better opportunity might be in store. Nothing surfaced, however, and for the next few years I bounced from one job to another, working in sales, framing, and a few other short-lived endeavors. Regardless, Jeannie and I adjusted to living in our townhouse. We also continued attending Christian Life Assembly, where we took part in ministry, developed new friendships, and matured in our faith.

I wasn't ready, though, to trust Jesus completely. In fact, when I think about these years, I imagine... *Jesus and me, walking down a fairway. I ramble on about my plans as His eyes roll in unconditional love, like a father being lectured by his middle-school know-it-all. I stop talking long enough to let Jesus choose an iron. We of course have yet to reach my ball.*

Arrogant, I know, but that was my mindset. I had a heavenly father but I still knew best. I believed God cared about the details of my life, and yet I felt compelled to walk a path of self-reliance, a path God would help me navigate but never choose or alter. I knew the way. I had all the skills to get there. Especially with His divine support.

But by 2009, neither God nor I had broken my string of jobs paying far too little. Disheartened, I resolved to stay home, unemployed, awaiting a position worth my while. Uneventful days turned quickly to drudgery. Repressed emotions hijacked my thoughts, and depression soon followed—deep, dark, unrelenting depression. I tried talking to psychiatrists but always wound up quitting, put off by their tactics. Always the same questions and onion-layer metaphors, prompting me to look within myself. I thought it all rubbish, though gladly accepted their prescriptions for pills.

One exception to this peel-and-prescribe therapy model was pastoral counseling at Christian Life Assembly. Like the psychiatrists I'd seen, this pastor listened to my woeful tale, but he made no attempt to uncover deeper issues. Instead he presented me with Scripture, challenged my self-pity, and encouraged me to take seriously God's will for my life. To pursue it, discover it, and fully embrace it. These, he counseled, were the first and most vital steps toward healing. His ideas at first annoyed me, but several sessions later I considered them honestly and thought maybe he was right. Maybe, just maybe, God did have a plan and purpose for my life. The possibility intrigued me. I just felt too down to care.

I had no ambition, no money, and no hope. When Jeannie would leave for work, I'd be lying on the couch, watching TV. When Jeannie would return, I'd be lying on the couch, watching TV. I sensed her frustration and the weariness of supporting a man who knew Jesus but refused to follow Him. I called myself a Christian, but until I lived by faith the joke was on me, and there was nothing funny about it.

Three years earlier, when we first began attending CLA, Jeannie recommitted her life to Jesus, trusting in His plan and provision. Since then she'd prayed for me to do the same, hoping that in God I'd find the peace, hope, and strength to move forward. But instead I only lingered near the edge of such commitment, unwilling to jump or place my life in God's hands.

He'd gotten my attention, shown me His love.

I just wasn't ready to return it.

A Word from Jeannie...

My faith was strong. Mark's was not.

I paused before walking upstairs, saw him lying on the couch, and said, "God is moving me along an unfamiliar path, and I'd really like you to be on this journey with me. I would love to do this 'God thing' together."

He said nothing in return, staring back with no discernable emotion.

In the months that followed, Mark's mental state showed no signs of improving, and I grew exceptionally weary. Depression also hurts loved ones, and Mark had been down far too long. I didn't deserve it or need it. And for the first time ever I thought about leaving.

We'd lost our home, the kids had moved out, my husband was a sloth, and I was already supporting myself financially. By worldly standards, I could justify leaving. But that's just it, I didn't want to live by worldly standards. I wanted to live for Jesus, and His perspective on marriage is entirely different.

One day in prayer, I squeezed my wedding ring and pushed God for answers.

"Should I stay, or should I go?"

His answer hit my heart with absolute clarity: Stay...and TRUST ME!

He then reminded me of two things: 1) my wedding vows; and 2) that in this world we have trouble but in Him we find peace. After this prayer I still struggled to like Mark, but I promised to never stop loving him. Every day was a challenge, but I kept believing God would heal my husband.

And my marriage.

Although depressed, I looked forward to choir and the CLA dramas, where I allowed myself to smile and laugh with other guys. With them, however, I built no close friendships and shared nothing on a personal level. We had good fun times, but ministry to me was only an outlet, a diversion, something to enjoy while I waited for what I really needed: a satisfying job.

In some respects, my faith had matured, but I still measured my worth by how people saw me professionally. And I felt terrified of being a nobody. The value of my life felt welded to my career and social status. Failing in business, declaring bankruptcy, losing my home, unresolved IRS battles; these festering wounds still motivated and defined me. Even as a Christian learning more about Jesus, I felt trapped in a cycle of emotional well-being, driven by employment and professional status. I knew my way to the top of the business community. I only needed God to bless my plans to return there.

It's okay; go ahead and laugh.

As more months passed without an offer, depression rooted in me to the point of self-loathing. I do not recall any suicidal thoughts, but meaningless days all but suffocated me. Like a sinister pendulum, my mind swung back and forth between paralyzing pity and scathing self-criticism. I detested what life had become, and I hated myself for still clutching the reigns, steering nowhere fast, merely turning circles in a pool of despair. Jeannie was hurting, both for me and because of me. How long she'd hang on was anybody's guess. And without her my life would truly be over.

My depression spilled over into 2010, but by God's grace, that's also when it ended. I was driving home from a psychiatrist appointment at which we'd done little more than discuss economics and refill my meds, when I developed an awareness that something must change. I'd known this before, cognitively, as a matter of principle. But on this day my soul seemed to shudder with awareness that my methods for healing had proven harmful and ineffective. My entire situation—from unemployment to depression to dependence on pills—was ridiculous and no longer tolerable. As I drove, memories surfaced, dots connected, until finally it hit me: God's way was the only way.

How could I have been so stubborn...so blind...so set in my ways? How?

My life up to now had been a lot like a roller coaster, with jubilant peaks and sudden descents dictating my emotions and mindset. Through it all God had revealed His love, but I'd either been too high or too low to receive it. I believed in Him, attended church, but never really gave Him my trust and devotion, never truly loved Him. To put it bluntly: God had been a convenience, valuable only when He fit my agenda. But now my roller coaster life simply wasn't ascending. Promising jobs eluded me. The market was dry. God had pinned me to the mat, and if I wanted to stand, He alone was the way.

Dancing through my mind were visions of my father and the church of my youth, where so many had believed in my potential. I recalled profitable decisions for which I alone had taken credit. I thought of stupid guy moments, cheating death by dumb luck, never acknowledging God's divine protection. I thought of Jeannie, the perky little ice-cream-cone-factory worker for whom I'd gone gaga in '78. After raising three children she'd grown only more beautiful, in body and spirit. She'd stood by me when many lesser women would have quit. Through Jeannie's faith God had preserved our marriage and kept my family intact. Not once had I thanked her or Him.

Arriving home, I laid down on the couch, staring at the ceiling. And like a bitter purge of heart, tears dampened my temples and tickled my ears as God's faithful provision came into sharp focus. I remembered the client who'd cared about my family when I'd called to inform him

I was closing the business. He could've exploded but responded with compassion, and in him I'd most likely seen Jesus. I thought of Cory and Patrick and their intriguing faith. I pictured home movers going out of their way to meet my every need. I thought of Jeannie's health club, the strong women in her life, and the changes I'd seen when she went all in with Jesus. I saw our Oil City neighbors, thought back on pastors and sermons and books I'd forgotten. Memory after memory pointed toward Jesus as He placed within my heart this message: "I forgive you. I love you. And I do have a plan. But until you lay down yours, you'll never walk in mine."

I sat up and said, "I can't do this anymore."

There they were again—the same five words I'd spoken to Jeannie in 2003.

The Bible says God is patient, wanting everyone to someday turn to Him. Well, this was my day, or better stated, His day. I twisted to the floor in a kneeling posture, folded my hands, and bowed my head. What I said next to Jesus I cannot transcribe, but I know it was a message of surrender and remorse, an affirmation that He is Lord, and a firm decision to trust in Him. My words were sincere. My motives pure. And my life thereafter belonged exclusively to Him.

Jeannie arrived home to find me sitting on the couch (already an improvement!) donning my first genuine smile in ages. When I shared what had happened, emotion overwhelmed us. For hours we shed tears and talked openly about my decision—what led to it, what it meant for me...for us. The burdens we faced remained as real and urgent as the day before, but now I knew without question God carried them and me in the palm of His hand, where I felt as safe and secure as I had years ago, tucked into bed in Oil City.

I'd trusted God like a child and become a better man for it.

From this day forward, I knew God had a plan for me to follow, not direct. I still took initiative but only in the knowledge that God was in control and would open or shut doors according to His will. I vowed only to seek Him, trust Him, and respond to opportunities He placed in my path. I didn't fully understand this change of heart within me, but that's the beauty of turning to Jesus; understanding is not required. God's ways are far beyond human comprehension. What He wanted from me was simply belief and a sincere confession of my need for Him. That's it. I didn't have to clean up my act or figure everything out. He loved me as I was, broken and confused. And I've never experienced a higher satisfaction.

Several weeks later I was waiting at a red light, listening to the rhythm of my clicking left turn signal. The radio was off. My mind was on work. And a feeling of peace washed over me. Since closing my business, I'd dismissed peaceful moments as anomalies, random times when my will to succeed overrode my fear of failure. But on this day my peace produced a deep assurance that I was headed in the right direction (never mind that I was about to turn left!). Seriously, I felt awakened to the fact that life was better, and it had nothing to do with money or prestige. My faith was real, and new life was emerging because of it. A mile later, weaving in and out of traffic, I yielded my peace to driving frustrations. But I'll never forget what occurred at that red light. A milestone moment in my life with Christ.

The personal changes that emerge from following Jesus are difficult to describe, but I can tell you two things: 1) they happen from the inside out; and 2) they have little to do with thou shalt or shalt not. After choosing life with Jesus, I didn't try hard to follow Biblical rules. I simply desired to know and please Him. My heart had been transformed to love Jesus, and inside I felt totally new. Perfect? Heck, no! Most days I still speak and behave like a knucklehead; just ask Jeannie. But in 2010, the compass of my life, my perspective on what matters most, became anchored to a bedrock of faith in Jesus Christ. And the difference it's made—the difference He's made—is simply indescribable.

As 2010 progressed, I opened my life—every ugly chapter and those yet to be written—to other Christian men I'd come to know and respect. I accepted counsel. I asked probing questions about life and faith and how to walk the walk. I listened carefully to sermons, read meaningful books, bought a new Bible, and studied it daily. God's word and relationships formed the core of my new being.

Life was no longer about me.

Yes, you read that correctly. Life was not about Mark Taylor. From one heartfelt prayer, Jesus washed the rust right out of my chest. And He not only closed my wounds, He healed them entirely. Life still hurt, I still faced problems, but only in the grace and strength of Jesus Christ. Pride had no place in my remodeled life. And to that point, I'll add this: Attending church does not prevent or heal pride.

I love church and believe it is vital to the life of every believer. But Christianity is about a relationship with Jesus, not buildings or steeples or religious formality. To help a man move beyond his pride, church must inspire and enhance his personal connection with Jesus. Today, I get it. But growing up and as a younger man, I thought of church like a club, a weekly gathering of believers in Jesus. In church I had friends and together we experienced reverence, formality, and Biblical teaching. My faith felt more academic than personal. And sad but true, my participation in church—singing, serving on committees, reading memorized responses—enhanced my self-image, stroked my ego. I did church on my terms, calling on Jesus only when needed. That's why pride, despite years of church involvement, gradually and deceptively entangled my soul. The fault, without question, was entirely mine.

And the old me would never have said that!

Again, let me emphasize, the changes in me were not my own doing or the result of a step-by-step religious program. They happened only because God created in me a genuine desire to do life His way. I still faced significant obstacles, including my previous tax evasion. Even today I deal with problems all the time, but not alone, not anymore. Never do I deal with even basic life decisions in my own strength or wisdom...or lack thereof.

Earlier I described an imaginary scene of telling Jesus my plans as we walked down a fairway. Today, I imagine us walking a similar fairway, but now His arm is wrapped around me as I hang on His words, soaking in all He wants to teach me. Like how not to hook my driver! Seriously, I never grow tired of hearing from Jesus, walking all of life's fairways with His arm guiding, correcting, and encouraging me forward.

Thank God I finally learned to listen.

A Word from Jeannie...

"Hey, Mom, I got my tattoo."

Far from a mother's worst nightmare, these words were certainly unnerving. I'd known Joanie, my youngest daughter, had been considering a tattoo, but I still felt tense when she announced the big reveal. Until I saw "Isaiah 43:1-3" on her foot. Permanently.

I'd shared these verses with her at a time when she'd been struggling. They talk about God's care and protection in all situations, which had meant the world to me in the wake of closing Mark's business. The second verse taught me that I'd sometimes walk through fire. I'd feel the heat, endure some pain, but through it all Jesus would guide me to find rest in Him. The fire of bankruptcy had rocked me to my core. But it also allowed me to live out the truth of God's word, and I can confidently say He brought beauty from ashes. Apparently He'd done the same in Joanie. The image on her foot reflected healing in her heart, and Momma really didn't mind this new tattoo.

In fact, it made me smile, inside and out.

I first heard Isaiah 43:1-3 while attending a study at Christian Life Assembly, where my faith expanded and matured in ways I'd never experienced. CLA's worship and messages seem to speak directly to me, and I cannot say enough about the friendships I've made there. To this day, wonderful women, including a female pastor on staff, surround me with care and speak messages of hope into my life. A hope anchored in the love and forgiveness of Jesus. So, to all readers, both men and women, I encourage you to find a church in your area where Jesus is honored and life in Him is emphasized. Christian Life Assembly is one of many great churches in this nation and around the world. Find one that fits you, participate, and experience with me the blessing of belonging to a family of Christ-followers.

I always believed Jesus to be the Son of God, but now I know Him personally. It's true: The creator of everything loves me and cares about the details of my life, no matter how small. He always hears, always listens. He may not answer in the ways I expect, but He faithfully responds on my behalf. The Bible makes clear He has a plan for my life, and He knows my needs before I even speak them.

When Mark's business closed, I was crying out for help, but no one seemed available. The country club crowd abandoned my family. Neighbor ladies kept me at arm's length with shallow smiles and conversation. So, I bottled my pain, dealt with it inwardly, privately. Until I met a woman who could sense I needed God. She invited me to hear her sing, but it was ultimately Jesus she wanted to share. Jesus transformed my life and then did the same in my husband and family. Oh, we're far from perfect. We still argue and complain and make plenty of mistakes. But we've discovered the freedom to live with hope, joy, and peace.

Even when life hurts.

How about you?

Improved Form and Function

CHAPTER EIGHT

S oon after making my commitment to Jesus, a promising position opened. If hired, I'd go to work for a supplier of solar energy panels, about which, despite all my building experience, I knew literally nothing. Nevertheless, I applied, interviewed, and landed the job. Did God have a hand in it? Absolutely. Just not for the reasons I expected.

The first few weeks were so confusing. My trainer told me the panels connected to the grid, and I just stared at him, wide-eyed. Yes, it was that embarrassing. But I soon caught on and developed a feel for the industry, selling panels to residential and business clients, even supervising installations. After only one year, I started managing the Mechanicsburg office, where my Christian faith was quickly tested.

An employee who reported directly to me was not working up to potential, and frankly his attitude stunk. The issue needed to be addressed as soon as possible. In my former years, I would have called my boss and the employee to a safe and impersonal group discussion. But this time I chose to do it God's way: man-to-man, heartfelt, honest. Though nervous, I brought this guy to my office, put my cards on the table, and respectfully asked him to change. He in turn yelled at me and walked out the door, and I thought: *Wow, God! That worked great.*

But my sarcasm proved premature.

The next morning this man walked back into my office and

declared he had something to say. I immediately thought he was about to resign. Wrong again. The first thing he said was that he'd gone home the night before and complained to his wife about me, but rather than commiserate she shared marriage concerns which the two of them talked about for hours. Next, this guy explained to me the difficult year he'd been having, saying that until his wife got honest he had no idea how much his hardships were affecting other people. He apologized, promised improvements in performance and attitude, and from that day forward we had a great relationship.

Wow, God! That worked great.

The same year, another test of faith came in the form of insurance costs. All of our personal coverage payments—life, home, auto, etc.—came due at the same time, totaling about $1,000. On top of rent and other living expenses, paying for insurance felt impossible.

One Sunday after church, a couple near our same age, whom we'd gotten to know through various ministry activities, invited us to lunch. Jeannie and I agreed to go, delighted by the opportunity to deepen this friendship. The meal was great, the conversation encouraging, and as we prepared to leave the restaurant, the husband said, "We've been praying for you guys, and we really believe God has asked us to give you this."

Into my hands he placed an envelope, likely containing some cash or a check, and honestly the gesture felt peculiar, almost surreal, arousing within me some resistance as well as adrenaline. Lost for words, Jeannie and I simply thanked our friends before going to our car, where we sat and stared at the sealed envelope. Moments later we prayed, then opened it, discovering within a check for $1,000. At once, we both cried, overwhelmed by God's provision.

I never knew people could be so compassionate just because God had dropped a name in their hearts. Our new friends had had no idea what their money would pay for or that what they'd felt moved to give was the exact amount we needed for insurance. This was no doubt God at work on our behalf. Not long after, Jeannie and I made a commitment to pay this gift forward. I hoped and prayed God would one day impress upon our hearts a financial need with such clarity. He eventually did, when our situation had improved enough to help a young couple with a similar gift.

God takes care of His people.

After two years of productive employment, Jeannie and I felt optimistic about my potential career in solar energy. I'd become knowledgeable in the industry and seemed poised for upward mobility. Our finances were stabilizing, we had money in savings, and when a larger energy company purchased my employer, I hoped the acquisition might lead to more and better opportunities. Sadly, that wasn't the case.

Within months of new ownership, installations decreased, and many clients stopped payments, causing cash receivables to exceed $1 million. Based on information from the new execs above me, I thought clients had simply stopped paying. I offered to help and got assigned to work with a new manager. He stayed in the office while I went to project sites, expecting to enforce collection. But what I discovered changed everything: faulty designs, shoddy workmanship, broken promises. Collect money for this! I was astonished by how bad the installations were. So, rather than enforce payments, I chose to make things right.

Some situations called for basic repairs, after which we did get paid. Others required us to tear out the work, forfiet the job, and refund money instead of collecting. The dealings were tense, the company pathetic, and I felt ashamed to be representing both.

One day the company president overheard me describing yet another flawed project. Clearly unconcerned, he said, "Just another party in our class action law suit." No compassion. No commitment.

No integrity. His words confirmed what I already knew: This company couldn't care less about its customers. Executives were content to promise big and deliver little. To disrupt lives with unprofessional installations, as long as they got paid. My heart ached with awareness that the projects I managed would never be backed by the professional quality I promised to clients. It simply knocked the wind right out of my sails.

I was making good money, driving company cars, and struggling daily with the ethical dilemma of lying to customers or resigning my position. More importantly I faced the spiritual challenge of listening to God. At times I wanted to ignore Him and stay the course, tempted again by the art of smoke and mirrors, but my personal character and commitment to Jesus meant too much. I just couldn't jeopardize them, tarnish them, not again. Another powerful test of faith had been placed before me. Would I really abandon stable income and advancement potential for issues of integrity…for God?

My career was gaining momentum. The potential existed to once again tread upon country club fairways, endearing myself to new movers and shakers, turning them on to the benefits of solar. But now I cared more about Jesus than money or image. If I entertained old habits, pride would overtake my faith. If I denied what I knew to be true, and reneged on my promise to listen to Jesus, I'd be placing my feet upon a slippery slope back to places I'd been and had no interest in returning. Jeannie and I prayed…and prayed…until God's direction became clear. Not through voices, dreams, or anything dramatic, but simply by our mutual, heartfelt impressions that I should resign. Without hesitation. Just walk away and trust Jesus.

I accepted this bold move as part of God's bigger plan, and yet it terrified me, which probably sounds contradictory given all my talk of faith. After all, shouldn't faith in Jesus overcome fear? In a word, yes.

The Bible has plenty to say about the power of faith over fear. But life gets scary, and even Christians feel afraid sometimes. What the Bible stresses is not the absence of fear but rather to never let fear eclipse faith, never allow it to gain the upper hand in our hearts and minds. We must respond in faith, despite fear. This defines courage, and God's men are called to be courageous. So, by faith alone, despite competing emotions, I prepared a resignation letter.

My supervisor already knew of my concerns, so handing him the letter would likely be harmless, and I expected his response to be calm and understanding. Nevertheless, I felt rattled, adrenaline spiking as I entered his office. My decision was final. I knew it was God's plan. But resigning in faith did little to diminish my hatred for being viewed as a quitter, by the company and my customers.

"Are you sure you want to do this?" my supervisor asked.

The question of the decade!

I took a moment to reflect, then said, "I think I need to."

"I understand," he responded. "I may leave here soon, myself."

I walked away affirmed, validated, and definitely relieved. For the next couple weeks, I tied up loose ends and prepared for departure. I even talked shop, when necessary, with the company owner—Mister Class Action Lawsuit. We discussed transition and reviewed projects in motion, but not once did he mention my resignation. Not once! I was the fourth highest member in the company structure, and he never even asked why I was leaving. Two weeks later my office was boxed, and my foreseeable tomorrows held only unemployment.

Let that sink in… After all I'd been through and aspired to achieve, I'd chosen unemployment over compromised character. You've read enough of my story to know that never in my previous life would I have considered such a move. Never. But that's what it's like to know Jesus. Hurts are healed, old habits take flight, and the lives they've destroyed are never rebuilt.

They're remodeled.

Let's revisit the Introduction… Remodeling begins with demolition. Out with the old, in with the new. Buildings are razed, spaces gutted, only to be recrafted with improved form and function. It's the essence of my trade. It is also, I believe, essential to life. Well, I hope by now you understand that a life can be demolished, stripped of flawed perspectives, toxic pride, and unhealthy behaviors. Personal wrecking balls take many forms. What matters is our choice to rise above the dust and rubble. But with what? Shards of broken life, or something else entirely?

The expression "pick up the pieces" is common during times of hardship, and in a practical sense it rings true and appropriate. But a broken man who reassembles himself will likely repeat the mistakes of his past. He may stand again, wiser, perhaps stronger, but with a similar disposition and behavioral patterns. Why? Because new men require new materials, from a divine creator.

God alone is the source of remodeled lives.

We must embrace His work. On the cross, and in life.

Every human being on the planet must personally decide to accept or reject Jesus Christ as Lord and Savior. And trust me: A casual, fence-straddling position doesn't cut it. I lived that way for decades, and though probably bound for heaven, I wasn't experiencing the transformational power of really knowing Jesus. Today I follow Him earnestly, and life is nowhere near the same. I still love the remodeling industry, but in Jesus I've learned to do everything in life with the form and function He remodeled in me. The essence of my trade is now the man that I am. If I'm not designing projects with a heart to love people, then I've missed the point of living entirely.

Ironically, while working in solar energy, I came close to achieving the goal I'd chased for years—recovering my life. I had a management position in a burgeoning industry, and my feet seemed set upon a path back to country club status. I'll never know for sure what would have happened had I'd stayed, but my future looked promising, and pride felt eager to pounce. I only needed to blur some facts, put profit before people, drop salesmanship lines, and manipulate outcomes. It was a game I'd mastered years ago, a game all too familiar, like riding a bike. But by God's grace something wiser and infinitely better had risen from my dust and rubble: a new man, built by and for Jesus.

One of many things nagging at my remodeled conscience was the mess I'd made of Joanie's senior year in high school, which just happened to coincide with losing my business. Over a decade had passed since then, but as a changed man, my heart would not rest until I apologized. I took her to lunch at a Mexican restaurant, where Daddy's girl listened to my heartfelt speech and then stared as if I'd fallen off my rocker. "Dad, it's okay! Really, it's fine." Apparently, she harbored no resentment, and senior year chaos was not the issue I'd expected it to be. As lunch continued I told her my story of faith in Jesus Christ, beginning with how hard I'd worked to get my old life back. Joanie's candid response: "Why did you even want it back?" Touché! Unexpected affirmation from the girl I'd intended to comfort.

As good as it felt to clear the air with my daughter, the hottest ember still smoldering in me was the sorrow I felt for putting Jeannie through such pain. Our journey had been long, sometimes grueling, and a heartfelt apology was long overdue. I think I'll let her tell you all about it.

A Word from Jeannie...

Since 2003, I've lost track of the times Mark sort of apologized.

A conversation might veer toward the business or something we'd lost because of it, and he'd say things like "I'm really sorry, Babe" or "Gosh, I'm so sorry about that." But his words never felt genuine and sometimes even smacked of a sales pitch. I'd just smile and thank him and continue on my way. I knew he wanted to mean them, and I understood the tremendous burden of guilt upon his shoulders. Worried about upsetting his fragile mental state, my heart just wouldn't allow me to challenge his sincerity. But believe me: A deep-seated anger still simmered in my soul, and his shallow apologies brought it quickly to mind.

The kids were grown and doing their thing. We were supposed to be enjoying our empty nest and saving for retirement, but we couldn't afford either. Any money I brought in went toward IRS penalties. For what Mark had done, not me! But when my anger came close to boiling over, I'd remember that my husband was mentally unfit and needed me to love him. For better or worse. For richer or poorer. In sickness and in health. No matter how furious I became, God always pushed wedding vows forward in my mind. And looking back I clearly see His protection and provision through those difficult years.

Then one day in 2014, over ten years since the business closed, Mark touched my heart with words I needed to hear. Sincere sentiments from my remodeled man. We were watching TV when he turned off the set and positioned himself near the edge of the couch, facing me. Then he took my hand as tears welled in his eyes, and said, "Jeannie, I'm so sorry for all that I put you through, put us through. From bankruptcy to losing the cars, losing our house, my mindset. Will you please forgive me?"

My heart pounded, my eyes dampened. The real deal...finally!

"Absolutely," I said, hugging him tightly.

The Bible says we must forgive others as God forgives us.

I knew it. Mark knew it.

And this day was a win, for us and Jesus.

Another Chance To Shine
CHAPTER NINE

"Hello, my name is Mark Taylor. May I please speak to the person responsible for the purchase of your lighting supplies?" I laugh every time I think of that old line. It's hard to imagine a more cringy introduction. But at that time, hawking light was a convenient first step toward rebuilding my life, my way. Ironically, many years later, it was another form of light, the one true light, that redefined my life's trajectory. The Bible says Jesus is the light of the world, and anyone who follows Him will never walk in darkness because His word illuminates what really matters. When this truth finally clicked for me, I overcame the aftermath of personal failure. I also discovered a new path forward.

After leaving solar energy no desirable positions opened, and my unemployment dragged on for months. Menial jobs held no appeal, and to be honest I didn't really need one. Jeannie's income was enough to make ends meet, allowing me the luxury of waiting out the right opportunity…or deciding to start another business. Oh, yes, you read that correctly. Unbeknownst to Jeannie, the more I prayed, the more I felt like God was restoring my passion and imparting fresh vision for the work I loved most.

I definitely did not want to misinterpret Jesus, and I was certainly on edge about a third swing at entrepreneurship. Therefore, I started by simply jotting notes, planning, dreaming, and all the while praying for His will to resonate. I promised to obey, even if He shut the door. Seriously, God was in control. On that point, I stood firmly resolved.

As this new idea developed, I experienced no desire to do construction or hire employees, thankfully, for the mere mention of employees to Jeannie might've landed me in the ER! At this stage in life I wanted to focus only on design and project management, like an architect equipped with years of experience in the home building industry. After all, there was very little I hadn't encountered in the remodeling world, and I understood how to work within budgets and hold contractors accountable. The crux of my emerging vision was to help clients achieve remodeling dreams by affordable means—for them and me.

My biggest investment would be in top-of-the-line software and the time required to learn it well. Beyond that I needed only to market myself, if you can imagine that! The business model was clean and efficient, with almost instant start up. I'd work from home, incur little or no debt, and hire no one. If I needed to quit, the process would be simple. Only one thing stood between me and the start of this God-ordained business. Telling my wife.

Step one: Take her to lunch. Well-prepared cuisine (aka pizza) might brighten her mood, and public exposure should prevent her from strangling me…or at least postpone it. She accepted my invitation. The plan was in motion.

Step two: Choose the right moment. The pizza had been served. We were two slices in. Conversation was light, smiles plentiful, and butterflies fluttered in my gut. The time had come to seize the day.

"Honey, I have an idea."

"Okay," she said, appearing unsure if I was about to propose ice cream or something more significant.

"I've given this a lot of thought, and… I'd like to start a design business."

Her face changed to a look of pure astonishment.

"We can begin for very little money," I continued. "Only software costs and some minor supplies. I'd really like to try it, just for a while, to see how things go."

My heart in my throat, I sensed someone approaching. Of all times! It turned out to be a contractor I'd known for many years. He'd just arrived at the restaurant and decided to say hello. We rushed through the typical guy banter greetings before rounding a corner into more sincere questions. He asked what I was doing career-wise, so I shared a brief synopsis of the business idea I was about to unpack for Jeannie.

He pointed at me, and said, "That's exactly what I need!"

Wow, what a God moment!

My old friend and I chatted a few minutes more, and as he walked away I looked at Jeannie. In her eyes I saw evidence of the same intuition I felt in my heart. From our faith perspective, God had intervened, creatively and with perfect timing. This contractor's response settled all debate…well, most of it anyway…about the wisdom and security of attempting another business. Jeannie and I still talked about the obvious risks and our smoldering emotions. But in the end we agreed to try this idea, and I felt thankful to have green lights from God and my wife. This time, I'd actually asked her.

I named my new company Diamond Design Consulting, and to date it's been very successful. All the lessons I've learned through hardship and faith are integrated into the business model. I did, however, retract my commitment to not hire anyone. This year Jeannie agreed to manage our home office, where we enjoy time together and operate with total financial transparency.

Diamond Design will always reflect my life remodeled. And I'm hopeful that maybe, just maybe, the light of Jesus in me will excite people's hearts as much if not more than the designs I enable.

In the opening chapter I shared how my dad and I differ regarding employment. But in many other ways I resemble my dad and always have. Since childhood I've desired to imitate his loose and good-humored way with people, his concern for others, his leadership, and his innate ability to make everyone around him better. And over the years, efforts to live out Dad's attributes have contributed much to me winning new clients, marketing myself, and convincing others that my crumbling life was somehow rosy. Even during the hardest times—closing the business, losing my home, the "great depression" of 2009—Dad's personal traits were the measuring stick by which I evaluated my health and wholeness.

What I failed to consider were the motives behind them.

Before Jesus remodeled my life, I tried to be like Dad for self-centered reasons that usually won the day. I'd help people get ahead but expect recognition. I'd emcee banquets so that I could get noticed. Success by others made me jealous, and blessing others was never a reward in itself. Everything I did had to benefit me. I hated this about myself, and on some level I did truly care about people, but getting ahead was an unbreakable habit. My motivation was pride, and you've just read where that got me.

After learning to trust Jesus, He changed me inside. I'm still wired with the same interests and talents, but my heart has flipped to a place of caring for others ahead of myself. Believe me, only God could be the architect of such radical remodeling! And what I've now discovered is that my father's characteristics no longer require work or even much thought. Out of my heart for others, they naturally flow. I guess that was Dad's secret all along.

Oh, you'll still never catch me working days in a cubicle, but when it comes to motivation or matters of the heart, my dad and I are united.

We are also united by our eternal destiny. Glenn R. Taylor, the man I most admire, is not long for this world. Alzheimer's has stolen his ability to appreciate this book or the lives he's influenced. But now I know, when my final day comes, I will embrace Dad again in a far better place.

Together forever. Two remodeled men.

Healthy and whole and standing in the presence of Jesus.

Thank you for reading His story.

We would love to hear from you.

HisStory.Mark@gmail.com

HisStory.Jeannie@gmail.com

HisStory.Chip@gmail.com

Or visit us online at

HisStoryMinistries.com

Life Remodeled

100

BEHIND THE STORY

When Chip first raised the idea of writing a book about my experiences, I thought it made sense and had the potential to impact lives. So, I was all for trying it. All for unveiling the devastating pain of losing in life. All for telling others what not to do. But as we discussed things in depth and with an eye toward writing, I began to realize the heartbeat of my story is not pain but victory.

Mine is a tale of triumph through faith in Jesus Christ. My hard lessons certainly matter because they set the stage, escalate tension, and help me relate to readers, especially those facing similar circumstances. But emphasizing hardship invites commiseration. To change lives, my story, the core of my message, has to be hope in Jesus Christ.

The world is full of people who've never heard about Jesus. I hope my story opens their eyes to how much He loves them. Others know about Jesus, perhaps even believe in Him, but refuse to let Him define their lives. For them, I hope my story illustrates the immeasurable value of living wholeheartedly for Jesus. Either way, I fully believe God brought Chip and I together to write this book. And if it leads even one person to know or grow in Christ, every minute we've invested has been worth it.

This book took nearly three years to write, but such was God's perfect timing. The process proved challenging but equally amazing. To us, completing the book felt like only step one in a journey that's just getting started.

My ultimate goal in life is to seek and fulfill God's purpose. Partnering with Chip to write Life Remodeled is now part of that mission. And we both pray God does more with it than either of us could ever hope or imagine.

Thank you for reading His story.

HisStoryMinistries.com

Study Guide

SESSION ONE: The Foundation

"Therefore everyone who hears these words of mine and puts them into practice is like a wise man who built his house on the rock. The rain came down, the streams rose, and the winds blew and beat against that house; yet it did not fall, because it had its foundation on the rock. But everyone who hears these words of mine and does not put them into practice is like a foolish man who built his house on sand. The rain came down, the streams rose, and the winds blew and beat against that house, and it fell with a great crash."
— Jesus (Matthew 7:24-27 NIV)

1. Take a minute to introduce yourself to the group. Briefly talk about your family, occupation, or anything else you feel comfortable sharing.

Have a group member(s) read aloud the introduction and first chapter of Life Remodeled. It's only a few pages. Then respond to the following questions.

2. Where were you raised, and what memories surface when you think of that place?

3. Mark's toilet seat story is always good for a laugh. What's a classic funny story from your family archives?

4. Describe your father and your relationship with him.

5. In what ways do you see your father in yourself?

6. In what ways are you different from your dad?

Take a minute to silently read Matthew 7:24-27. Underline any words or phrases that stand out for you personally.

7. In this tale of the wise and foolish builders, what or who does the rock represent? What about the harsh weather?

8. What does this story teach us about foundations in life?

For Next Session: Read Chapter Two: The Fracture
Reflect on your personal foundation and how it contributes to the man you are today.

SESSION TWO: The Fracture

Listen to advice and accept instruction, that you may gain wisdom in the future. Many are the plans in the mind of a man, but it is the purpose of the LORD that will stand. (Proverbs 19:20-21 ESV)

1. What was your first teenage, gas-money job?

2. What or who has influenced your career path to date?

3. Have you ever desired to start your own business, and if so how did you respond?

4. When have you experienced life moving too fast, and how did you cope with or change things?

Read again Mark's words from Chapter Two: "To embrace risk in pursuit of one's dream is a noble undertaking. What I didn't understand is that determination alone will fail the dreamer. Required is thoughtful persistence. No matter how passionately a man desires to achieve his goals, patience, humility, and a willingness to learn must underscore his drive, providing a new and firm foundation upon which to anchor his pursuit."

5. What do you think about Mark's claims, and how might this logic apply to your life?

Take a minute to silently read Proverbs 19:20-21. Underline any words or phrases that stand out for you personally.

6. How does advice differ from instruction?

7. What connection do you see between these verses and Mark's choices?

8. What connection do you see between these verses and your life, past or present?

For Next Session: Read Chapter Three: The Climb
Reflect on one decision you are currently considering and decide if wise counsel is called for. To whom might you turn?

SESSION THREE: The Climb

"For whoever wants to save their life will lose it, but whoever loses their life for me will find it. What good will it be for someone to gain the whole world, yet forfeit their soul? Or what can anyone give in exchange for their soul? For the Son of Man is going to come in his Father's glory with his angels, and then he will reward each person according to what they have done."
— Jesus (Matthew 16:25-27 NIV)

1.   What is one of your favorite worldly possessions, and why is it special to you?

2.   Changing houses is a major theme in Chapter Three. What thoughts or feelings surface when you recall the moves in your life? And if you've ever built a home, how well can you relate to what Mark and Jeannie experienced?

After accepting a position at Zimmerman Homes, Mark says: "If I wasn't on the job physically, I was there in my mind, spending every waking hour thinking and worrying. My position had no time clock, no punching out for the day. I managed the schedules of all other employees and carried the burden of satisfying customers. The success of our office and the projects we undertook rested squarely on my shoulders. Stress escalated far above what I'd experienced at Joy Manufacturing, while my pay checks, mind you, were thirty percent less. For extra cash, I refereed wrestling with time I didn't have. I became short-tempered, a bristly man at work and home. A grouch of a dad. A distant husband."

3. To what extent and in what specific ways can you relate to Mark's situation?

Near the end of Chapter Three, Mark, now an executive leader at a major corporation, considers moving his family to Exton, PA, in pursuit of higher status and income. He describes himself as "blinded by another opportunity."

4. To what was Mark blind, and have you ever felt the same?

5. When has enthusiasm ever led you to make an impulsive or unwise decision?

Take a minute to silently read Matthew 16:25-27. Underline any words or phrases that stand out for you personally.

6. In the first verse, Jesus is not talking about physical life or death. So, what is this life we either save or lose for Him?

7. Jesus asks: "What good will it be for someone to gain the whole world, yet forfeit their soul?" Answer His question.

8. How do these verses relate to Mark's story so far? What about yours?

For Next Session: Read Chapter Four: My Business, Period
                            Reflect daily on your current priorities in
                            light of Matthew 16:25-27.

SESSION FOUR: My Business, Period

As iron sharpens iron, so one person sharpens another. (Proverbs 27:17 NIV)

1. In Chapter Four, Mark attempts to teach Jeannie how to golf. Have you ever tried to teach or share your hobby with a spouse or significant other? How did things go?

As the proud owner of Taylor Home Remodeling, Mark says: "I bought out Greg's share in the company. For me, the move symbolized achievement, a rite of passage to exclusive ownership and decision making. To put it bluntly: I'd proven myself successful and saw little value in continuing to receive Greg's counsel. My business. My decisions. Period."

2. It's easy to criticize Mark's arrogant tone, but to what extent can you empathize with his desire to stand alone, and have you ever felt likewise?

3. How would you describe the fatal flaw in Mark's logic?

4. What did you think and feel when Mark fired his right-hand man and accountant for not saying what he wanted to hear?

5. Why is it healthy for others to sometimes challenge our thoughts and decisions?

6. Was it wise for Mark to keep his best foot forward despite inner turmoil; why or why not?

Take a minute to silently read Proverbs 27:17. Underline any words or phrases that stand out for you personally.

7. In everyday language, what does it look like for one person to sharpen another, and what qualities must exist in each of them?

8. The sharpening of people in a healthy relationship is mutual, meaning both grow from knowing one another. Do you agree; why or why not?

For Next Session: Read Chapter Five: The Collapse
Identify a sharpening relationship in your life and thank that person. If you don't have one, think of a friendship worth deepening, and take a first step.

SESSION FIVE: The Collapse

AWhen the men were returning home after David had killed the Philistine, the women came out from all the towns of Israel to meet King Saul with singing and dancing, with joyful songs and with timbrels and lyres. As they danced, they sang: "Saul has slain his thousands, and David his tens of thousands." Saul was very angry; this refrain displeased him greatly. "They have credited David with tens of thousands," he thought, "but me with only thousands. What more can he get but the kingdom?" And from that time on Saul kept a close eye on David. (1 Samuel 18:6-9 NIV)

1. Where and how do you experience rest and relaxation?

As Israel's first king, Saul experiences military success but fails to obey God's commands. Consequently, God appoints young David to replace him, but not right away. In fact, the transition takes several years, during which Saul grows increasingly fearful and jealous of David. Overcome with anxiety, Saul attempts to manipulate and kill him, ultimately pursuing David through caves and harsh terrain. By God's grace, David not only eludes Saul but also gives up two easy chances to kill him, choosing instead to honor God above retaliation. In the end, Saul fails to eliminate David, and eventually dies while at war with the Philistines. (Paraphrase of 1 Samuel 9-31)

2. What similar themes can you identify between King Saul's downfall and Mark's collapse in Chapter Five?

3. What causes you stress and how do you deal with it, especially when escape is not an option?

Mark says: "Emotional pain and intolerable guilt crippled me, gutted my life of all that once defined Mark Taylor. What sleep I managed happened only alone, on the couch, in the wee hours of the morning. Despite taking prescription Ambien, I spent most nights writhing and wrestling with what-if scenarios nothing short of sheer terror, much worse than the nightmares that haunted my slumber. I felt physically sick, mentally imprisoned."

4. To what extent can you identify with these words, in full or in part?

5. What have been the hardest days of your life so far, and how did they shape the man you are today?

Take a minute to silently read 1 Samuel 18:6-9. Underline any words or phrases that stand out for you personally.

6. Saul says he is angry, but what other emotions help to fuel his anger?

7. How should followers of Jesus respond to success by others?

8. Should a Christian ever fear or envy the achievements of others; why or why not?

For Next Session: Read Chapter Six: Dust and Rubble
Pay specific attention to your anxiety. How do you carry it physically? What thoughts drive it up or down? What choices or behaviors does it impact?

SESSION SIX: Dust and Rubble (Part One)

Do not be deceived: God cannot be mocked. A man reaps what he sows. Whoever sows to please their flesh, from the flesh will reap destruction; whoever sows to please the Spirit, from the Spirit will reap eternal life. Let us not become weary in doing good, for at the proper time we will reap a harvest if we do not give up. (Galatians 6:7-9 NIV)

1. Talk briefly about your gardening experience. Who among you has the greenest thumb, and who has the potential to kill artificial plants?

2. If you sow an apple seed, it will always (assuming proper care) produce an apple tree. Why does this matter in a discussion about life?

3. Talk about one of your best decisions; what led to it, and how it impacted your life.

4. What type of thoughts often lead to regrettable decisions?

Mark says: "...as days clicked by and a new normal took shape, I slipped back to a pattern of stuffing my pain and operating publicly as if things were fine, always playing the salesman. My default setting was to market myself, and more than ever I had to open the right doors, impress the right people."

5. What concerns you the most about Mark's perspective?

6. How would you describe your default setting, and how might others describe it?

Take a minute to silently read Galatians 6:7-9. Underline any words or phrases that stand out for you personally.

7. Men with selfish motives often experience prosperous living, so why do these verses speak of reaping destruction?

8. What does it really mean to do good, and why might one become weary in it?

For Next Session: Review Chapter Six: Dust and Rubble
                          Pay specific attention to the motivation of
                          your heart. Be brutally honest about
                          why you are choosing to think, speak, or act a
                          certain way—even if it's Christian in nature.

SESSION SEVEN: Dust and Rubble (Part Two)

"Come to me, all you who are weary and burdened, and I will give you rest. Take my yoke upon you and learn from me, for I am gentle and humble in heart, and you will find rest for your souls. For my yoke is easy and my burden is light."

— Jesus (Matthew 11:28-30 NIV)

1. Mark still laughs about his lighting supply sales pitch. Take a minute to share one of your funny work stories.

After discussing bankruptcy with his father, Mark says: "Later, I cried about disappointing Dad and feeling such indignation. Whether he fully understood my situation did not matter. Sharing life with him was always important, validating, the one thing that seemed to solidify the reality of anything significant. I suppose in every man lives the boy he used to be, pursuing warmth and praise from a loving father. In this world or the next."

2. Reading these sentiments, what stands out to you personally, and why?

Crushed by his employer, Mark says: "Stressed beyond measure, I felt little support and was reminded almost daily that corporate bonuses hinged upon my team's ability to settle enough houses before year end. Fortunately my salespeople and managers were excellent, up to the task of meeting corporate demands in a burgeoning market. We settled eighteen different homes in the fourth quarter alone. Under intense pressure, we rose to the occasion, and I felt proud of myself and my team. Anxiety, however, continued taking its toll."

3. How is your relationship with your boss? If you are your own boss, answer anyway.

4. Have you ever felt compelled to continue doing something that was breaking you, and if so why did you feel that way?

5. Why do most men bottle their emotions, and what are the risks?

Take a minute to silently read Matthew 11:28-30. Underline any words or phrases that stand out for you personally.

6. How does Jesus describe Himself in these verses, and how does His description align with your concept of God?

7. In what specific ways does Jesus use the imagery of a yoke to teach about living in relationship with Him?

8. Jesus promises rest for your soul, an easy yoke, and a light burden. Does that mean life with Jesus is never difficult; why or why not?

For Next Session: Read Chapter Seven: New Beginnings
Memorize Matthew 11:28, "Come to me, all you who are weary and burdened, and I will give you rest." Repeat these words during stressful moments, and note the results.

SESSION EIGHT: New Beginnings (Part One)

"For I know the plans I have for you," declares the LORD, "plans to prosper you and not to harm you, plans to give you hope and a future. 12 Then you will call on me and come and pray to me, and I will listen to you. 13 You will seek me and find me when you seek me with all your heart." (Jeremiah 29:11-13 NIV)

1. When preparing for a trip, do you plan every detail or fly by the seat of your pants? If married, how well does this go over with your spouse?

2. How did Mark's perspective of the townhouse differ from Jeannie's?

3. How would you describe the difference between self-initiative and self-sufficiency? Which one leaves room for God, and how does it operate together with faith?

4. Mark discovers in his colleague, Cory, the impressiveness of humility. What does Mark mean, and why does this viewpoint surprise him?

Mark says: "I had a heavenly father but I still knew best. I believed God cared about the details of my life, and yet felt compelled to walk a path of self-reliance, a path God would help me navigate but never choose or alter. I knew the way. I had all the skills to get there.

Especially with His divine support."

5. It's easy to criticize Mark's perspective, but can you honestly do so without any hypocrisy; why or why not?

About his pastoral counselor, Mark says: "He presented me with Scripture, challenged my self-pity, and encouraged me to take seriously God's will for my life. To pursue it, discover it, and fully embrace it. These, he counseled, were the first and most vital steps toward healing."

6. Given these same suggestions, how would you respond or apply them to your life?

Take a minute to silently read Jeremiah 29:11-13. Underline any words or phrases that stand out for you personally.

7. If God's plan is to prosper and not harm His people, why does life still hurt?

8. What does it mean to do something wholeheartedly, and what does God say about seeking Him that way?

For Next Session: Review Chapter Seven: New Beginnings
Reflect upon your favorite childhood
activities, those things you chose to
do for hours on end. Are they still in your
life? Should they be? What might they reveal
about God's unique plan and purpose?

SESSION NINE: New Beginnings (Part Two)

When pride comes, then comes disgrace, but with humility comes wisdom.
(Proverbs 11:2 NIV) *Pride goes before destruction, a haughty spirit before
a fall.* (Proverbs 16:18 NIV) *Before a downfall the heart is haughty, but
humility comes before honor.* (Proverbs 18:12 NIV)

1. Take a minute to talk about something you are proud of.

2. What's the difference between being proud of something and
   being a prideful person?

Mark says: "In some respects, my faith had matured, but I still
measured my worth by how people saw me professionally. And I felt
terrified of being a nobody. The value of my life felt welded to my
career and social status… Even as a Christian learning more about
Jesus, I felt trapped in a cycle of emotional well-being, driven by
employment and professional status. I knew my way to the top of the
business community. I only needed God to bless my plans to return
there. It's okay; go ahead and laugh."

3. Why do you think Mark gives permission to laugh?

4. Is it okay for a Christian man to identify strongly with his
   profession, or even take pride in his work? Why or why not, and
   how does that differ from what Mark is experiencing?

Mark says: "And sad but true, my participation in church—singing, serving on committees, reading memorized responses—enhanced my self-image, stroked my ego. I did church on my terms, calling on Jesus only when needed."

5. How well does Mark's confession correlate with your answers to question two?

6. Why does God oppose the proud?

Take a minute to silently read the Proverbs printed above. Underline any words or phrases that stand out for you personally.

7. In each of these verses, what truth rings clear about pride and humility?

8. Humility does not mean passiveness or wimpiness. So, then, what does humility look like in a strong, assertive man?

For Next Session: Review Chapter Seven: New Beginnings
Reflect upon your own mortality. That may
sound morbid, but death's inevitability
sharpens our awareness of what matters
most in life and how our time is being spent.

SESSION TEN: New Beginnings (Part Three)

But now, this is what the LORD says—he who created you, Jacob, he who formed you, Israel: "Do not fear, for I have redeemed you; I have summoned you by name; you are mine. When you pass through the waters, I will be with you; and when you pass through the rivers, they will not sweep over you. When you walk through the fire, you will not be burned; the flames will not set you ablaze. For I am the LORD your God, the Holy One of Israel, your Savior; I give Egypt for your ransom, Cush and Seba in your stead." (Isaiah 43:1-3 NIV)

1. What is your favorite war movie?

2. What comes to mind when most men think of surrender?

3. In what ways, if any, does your life feel like a personal war?

After years of fighting for his life, Mark says: "I was driving home from a psychiatrist appointment, at which we'd done little more than discuss economics and refill my meds, when I developed an awareness that something must change. I'd known this before, cognitively, as a matter of principle. But on this day my soul seemed to shudder with awareness that my methods for healing had proven harmful and ineffective. My entire situation—from unemployment to depression to dependence on pills—was ridiculous and no longer tolerable. As I drove, memories surfaced, dots connected, until finally it hit me: God's way was the only way."

4. Up to this point, what methods of healing had Mark tried, and what were the results?

5. What does Mark mean by God's way, and what questions do you have about following Jesus?

Mark says: "I'd trusted God like a child and become a better man for it."

6. What is unique about childlike faith, and how does it pertain to Christian manhood?

Take a minute to silently read Isaiah 43:1-3. Underline any words or phrases that stand out for you personally.

7. How do these verses characterize the type of relationship God desires with you?

8. What might change if you trusted these words with childlike faith? Be specific.

For Next Session: Read Chapter Eight: Improved Form and Function
Take time to prayerfully consider what God may be asking you to lay down so His plan can rise up. What's stopping you?

SESSION ELEVEN: Improved Form and Function

And [Jesus] died for all, that those who live should no longer live for themselves but for him who died for them and was raised again. So from now on we regard no one from a worldly point of view. Though we once regarded Christ in this way, we do so no longer. Therefore, if anyone is in Christ, the new creation has come: The old has gone, the new is here! (2 Corinthians 5:15-17 NIV)

1. Diagnosable phobias range from expected (snakes or heights) to bizarre (balloons or hair). What scares you?

Mark says: "I was making good money, driving company cars, and struggling daily with the ethical dilemma of lying to customers or resigning my position. More importantly I faced the spiritual challenge of listening to God. At times I wanted to ignore Him, stay the course, tempted again by the art of smoke and mirrors, but my personal character and commitment to Jesus meant too much. I just couldn't jeopardize them, tarnish them, not again. Another powerful test of faith had been placed before me. Would I really abandon stable income and advancement potential for issues of integrity...for God?"

2. What does Mark fear in this situation, and why is he tempted to ignore God?

3. Why is courage essential to living by faith, and what causes some men to misunderstand this?

Mark says: "Personal wrecking balls take many forms. What matters is our choice to rise above the dust and rubble. But with what? Shards of broken life, or something else entirely? The expression "pick up the pieces" is common during times of hardship, and in a practical sense it rings true and appropriate. But a broken man who reassembles himself will likely repeat the mistakes of his past. He may stand again, wiser, perhaps stronger, but with a similar disposition and behavioral patterns. Why? Because new men require new materials, from a divine creator. God alone is the source of remodeled lives. We must embrace His work. On the cross, and in life."

4. Have you ever experienced a personal wrecking ball, and how are you different because of it?

5. Do you agree that a broken man who reassembles himself will likely repeat the mistakes of his past; why or why not?

6. Mark emphasizes changing from the inside out. What does he mean, and why is this important to understanding faith in Jesus?

Take a minute to silently read 2 Corinthians 5:15-17. Underline any words or phrases that stand out for you personally.

7. What correlation do you see between these verses and Mark's faith journey?

8. When a man is created new in Christ, what changes, and what doesn't?

9. What or who led you to Jesus? Or, what questions or hesitations do you still have?

For Next Session: Read Chapter Nine: Another Chance to Shine
Reflect upon the personal impact Mark's
story and this study have had on you. Also,
take at least one courageous act of faith,
no matter how small it might seem, and note
the outcome.

SESSION TWELVE: Another Chance To Shine

Take delight in the LORD, and he will give you the desires of your heart. Commit your way to the LORD; trust in him and he will do this: He will make your righteous reward shine like the dawn, your vindication like the noonday sun. (Psalm 37:4-6 NIV)

1. What are some things you really enjoy?

Mark says: "...the more I prayed, the more I felt like God was restoring my passion and imparting fresh vision for the work I loved most."

2. After reading these words and knowing Mark's story, what can you conclude about a heart's desires before and after Jesus?

3. What changed in Mark, his passion or vision, and why is this distinction significant?

Mark says: "I definitely did not want to misinterpret Jesus, and I was certainly on edge about a third swing at entrepreneurship. Therefore, I began by simply jotting notes, planning, dreaming, and all the while praying for His will to resonate. I promised to obey, even if He shut the door. Seriously, God was in control. On that point, I stood firmly resolved."

4. How can a guy like Mark, so ambitious and driven, be at peace with God in control?

Writing about the contractor who approached him during lunch,

Mark says: "He asked what I was doing career-wise, so I shared a brief synopsis of the business idea I was about to unpack for Jeannie. He pointed at me, and said, 'That's exactly what I need!' Wow, what a God moment!"

5. What does Mark mean by a God moment, and when have you experienced one?

Mark concludes: "Diamond Design will always reflect my life remodeled. And I'm hopeful that maybe, just maybe, the light of Jesus in me will excite people's hearts as much if not more than the designs I enable."

6. What truth has Mark learned about life and employment, and have you ever felt likewise in your daily grind?

Take a minute to silently read Psalm 37:4-6. Underline any words or phrases that stand out for you personally.

7. What does it mean to delight in the Lord, and how does that differ from simply believing in Him?

8. How did Mark's story and this study impact your life?

Next Steps: Read God's Word, every day.
                   Commit to know Jesus. Follow Him closely
                   and discover in Him the desires of your heart.
                   Continue to meet with the men in your group
                   and explore other opportunities to grow in
                   friendship and faith.
                   Your life remodeled awaits!

Have thoughts about this study?
Want to share a story about God's work in your life?
We would love to hear from you!

HisStoryMinistries.com